Collins

KEY CONCEPTS IN
Business Studies

GW00569748

Karen Borrington and Peter Stimpson

William Collins' dream of knowledge for all began with the publication of his first book in 1819. A self-educated mill worker, he not only enriched millions of lives, but also founded a flourishing publishing house. Today, staying true to this spirit, Collins books are packed with inspiration, innovation and practical expertise. They place you at the centre of a world of possibility and give you exactly what you need to explore it.

Collins. Freedom to teach

Published by Collins
An imprint of HarperCollins*Publishers*
77 – 85 Fulham Palace Road
Hammersmith
London
W6 8JB

Browse the complete Collins catalogue at
www.collins.co.uk

© HarperCollins*Publishers* Limited 2013

10 9 8 7 6 5 4 3 2 1

ISBN-13 978 0 00 752196 8

Karen Borrington and Peter Stimpson assert their moral rights to be identified as the authors of this work.

British Library Cataloguing in Publication Data
A Catalogue record for this publication is available from the British Library

Commissioned by Alexandra Riley
Project managed by Sue Chapple
Production by Emma Roberts

Typeset by Jouve India Private Limited Illustrations by Ann Paganuzzi
Edited by Philippa Boxer and Sue Chapple
Proof read by Pat Dunn
Indexed by Jane Coulter
Photo research by Shelley Noronha
Concept design by Angela English
Cover design by Angela English

Printed and bound in China.

With special thanks to Denry Machin and Catherine Wright for carrying out a comprehensive peer review of this text.

Acknowledgements
The publishers wish to thank the following for permission to reproduce photographs. Every effort has been made to trace copyright holders and to obtain their permission for the use of copyright material. The publishers will gladly receive any information enabling them to rectify any error or omission at the first opportunity.

Cover & p 1 Akindo/iStockphoto; p 9 David Porter Peterborough UK/Getty Images; p 15 KingWu/iStockphoto; p 20 Zenith Bank plc; pp 21, 30, 35, 46, 65, 70, 76, 146, 150, 161, 165 Shutterstock.com; pp 24, 95, 154, 196 AFP/Getty Images; p 27 Sergey Nivens/Shutterstock.com; pp 51, 91, 129, 191, 206 iStockphoto; pp 62, 82, 169, 176 Bloomberg via Getty Images; p 79 Katherine Welles/Shutterstock.com; pp 103, 120, 126 Getty Images; p 105 Radu Bercan/Shutterstock.com; p 108 Studiomode/Alamy; p 112 Adidas via Getty images; p 116 Ian Dagnall Computing/Alamy; p 141 David Arts/Shutterstock.com; p 159 Robert Convery/Alamy; p 167 Hindustan Times/Getty Images

Contents

Business objectives

An objective is an aim or target for the future. Long-term business objectives are used to establish targets for all divisions and departments. This helps coordination towards achieving the overall aim of the business. Without clear objectives, management cannot decide on appropriate business strategies.

Why set objectives?

The main reasons for setting objectives include:

➤ To give the organisation a sense of direction or focus

➤ To inform employees of what they should aim to achieve

➤ To help in assessing 'success' or 'failure' when compared with actual performance

➤ To encourage investors, as clear objectives should lead to appropriate strategies for the future

➤ To communicate to external stakeholders such as shareholders and customers.

Why should objectives be SMART?

Business objectives must be clear and effective. They must be SMART:

S = Specific to the business, e.g. to increase market share to 15% of the UK car market for a car manufacturer

M = Measurable, usually in quantitative terms so that comparisons can be made with actual performance

A = Achievable, because objectives that it may be impossible to achieve will not provide direction and motivation to employees

R = Realistic and relevant to the people trying to achieve them

T = Time specific – there should be a time limit for achieving them.

Management by Objectives (MBO)

This is the process of extending the overall objectives of the business into departmental (or operating) objectives. Everyone within the business has set objectives that contribute to the overall business objectives. It attempts to ensure that everyone is well focused on a common corporate objective.

Factors influencing business objectives

Age of the business: If it is recently established, survival will be the key aim. It is important to establish early stability.

Economic conditions: During an economic boom most businesses aim to increase sales and profit. During a recession, survival or maintaining market share might become more important.

Private or public sector: Owners of private sector businesses expect a return on their investment, so profitability will be an objective. Public sector businesses, owned by the government, may have other aims, such as to deliver an effective service.

Legal structure: In public limited companies there is a divorce between ownership and control, and directors may put growth above total profitability. Sole traders may consider maintaining independence as most important.

Culture of the business: Many social enterprises will typically have three objectives – profit (reinvested to improve the product or service), social benefit and environmental protection. Large public limited companies might aim only to increase profits to raise returns to shareholders.

Potential conflicts between objectives

Conflicts can occur in a number of different ways, such as:

➤ Ethical or environmental protection issues might conflict with a profit objective.

➤ Profit in the short term might conflict with growth and profit objectives in the longer term. For example, investing capital for long-term expansion may reduce profitability in the shorter term.

Vision statements and mission statements

Many businesses develop vision and mission statements. They are not SMART so are of limited operational use in managing a business but they do state in general terms what a business hopes to achieve.

A **vision statement** expresses where a business 'wants to be' and is mostly for external stakeholders. It sums up the central purpose and values of the organisation.

A **mission statement** is more detailed than a typical vision statement and more focused on what the business actually intends to do. For example, part of the mission statement of easyJet is: 'To provide our customers with safe, good value, point-to-point air services. To offer a consistent and reliable product and fares appealing to leisure and business markets on a range of European routes.'

Advantages and drawbacks of a mission statement

Advantages	Disadvantages
• Tells shareholders and potential investors what the business 'is about'	• Can be very general and just 'wishful thinking'
• Creating a mission statement can bring senior managers together	• Does not provide SMART objectives
• Provides a sense of purpose to managers and other employees	• May need to be revised frequently if the nature of the business changes

Case study

Air Mauritius has been hit by the global economic crisis and rising fuel prices. This has reduced its profitability. The directors have launched a new vision statement (to 'become the leading airline to Mauritius and the Indian Ocean'), established revised core objectives and set out new strategies. New operational objectives include increasing capacity, 'relentless' cost reductions and re-balancing growth towards short-to-medium-term routes. New strategies designed to achieve these objectives include: replacing old aircraft with more fuel-efficient types; opening a new route and offering more competitive flight prices on key routes.

Summary

Objectives provide direction and focus to business activity and can be communicated to employees. Business operating objectives need to be 'SMART'. Vision statements and mission statements project the overall ambitions of the business but they have limited operational use.

Business plans

A business plan is a document containing the objectives of a business and important details about its operations, marketing and finance. It is written when an entrepreneur is intending to set up a new business. It communicates essential information to investors and lenders. An existing business which is planning a significant change, such as selling abroad for the first time, is also likely to produce a business plan.

Preparing a business plan

When preparing a business plan – see opposite for example – the entrepreneur must plan carefully for the first years of operation. This means considering many factors, including:

➤ What products or services will I provide?

➤ Which consumers am I targeting?

➤ How will I market the products or services?

➤ What will be the main costs and will enough products be sold, or services provided, for the business to be profitable?

➤ Where will the business be located and is this suitable?

➤ What equipment will be needed and should this be purchased or hired?

➤ How many employees will be required?

Benefits to entrepreneurs

There are several benefits from this planning process:

➤ It might become obvious that the business idea will not succeed and the entrepreneur may consider an alternative.

Business plan for Jim's Garden Designs Ltd.

Name of business	Jim's Garden Designs Ltd
Legal structure	Private limited company
Business aims	To provide a quality garden design and landscaping service
	To make a return on capital of at least 15%
Service provided	Garden design and landscaping service
Price	Average expected: £500 for a design, £300 per day landscaping/gardening services
Market segment	Home owners in middle and high income areas
Market research	Interviews with home owners in the area
	Local competition and national expenditure on garden services
Human Resources	Two directors (the owners) – the only employees initially. Part-time employee if customer numbers above forecast
Business owners	Jim Lee: Degree in Garden Design; 10 years' experience with major garden centre
	Gowri Davies: 8 years' experience as gardening assistant with Local Government Parks Authority
Operational details and business costs	Main suppliers – P & P Garden Equipment Hire Co.
Fixed costs	£50,000 per year
Variable costs	Rocks, fencing, compost and other materials used
Business location	Office premises – Jim Lee's home address
Main equipment	Second-hand gardening equipment – £6,000 Second-hand van – £10,000
Forecast profit	See financial appendix. Summary: In Year 1, total costs forecast to be £90,000 with revenue of £125,000. Predicted profit = £35,000
	Break-even: 25 customers per year
Cash flow	See financial appendix. Due to high set-up and promotion costs there will be negative cash flow in the first year.
Finance	Share capital: £10,000 invested by J. Lee; £5,000 invested by G. Davies
	Request to bank for a further £4,000 + overdraft arrangement of £2,000 per month

➤ A well-constructed plan makes raising finance easier. Banks will want to see details of the entrepreneur, the business idea, the costs involved, the potential profit and an estimate of likely cash flows.

➤ Planning makes the entrepreneur think carefully about the resources needed and how they will be obtained.

➤ The plan includes projections and budgets for the first months and years of operation. By comparing these with actual results, the owner can assess progress.

No guarantee of success

A business plan will not guarantee success:

➤ It might not have been based on up-to-date or accurate, professionally collected market research data.

➤ Subsequent changes in the external environment can be significant, for example an economic recession, new competitors or changes in customers' tastes.

➤ Success of new businesses depends on many other factors, such as the competence of the entrepreneur, the quality of the employees and the cost and availability of materials.

Existing businesses

Existing businesses also need to plan ahead. Long-term corporate planning is key to ensuring that new strategies achieve long-term objectives.

Benefits of corporate planning for existing businesses include:

➤ Takes a long-term view of the strategic options.

➤ Can help with effective control and evaluation.

➤ Ensures coordination between departments.

➤ Motivates departments to achieve the objectives.

➤ Clarifies what resources will be needed in the future.

Limitations for existing businesses include:

➤ Can become an end in itself rather than a means of improving business performance.

➤ Can be very time-consuming.

➤ Can be too rigid and inflexible.

Case study

The owners of the Riverside Café dreamed of it being a leading gourmet café-restaurant. Their business plan highlighted the sizeable target market and the lack of nearby competition. Financial forecasts showed a potential 75% gross profit margin and £23,000 net profit by the end of year 3.

The plan gave details about the range of drinks and food items that the café was going to provide and the emphasis on customer service, and a profile of typical customers was included. The business plan helped the owners obtain the necessary long-term bank loan of £60,000.

That was two years ago. The owners are delighted with the success of their business but with the continuing economic difficulties, they have had to lower the profit target for year 3.

Summary

A business plan for a new business start-up contains key information about the entrepreneur, the business idea and the ways in which it will be marketed and financed. However carefully prepared, a business plan cannot guarantee success.

Business size & growth

Business size refers to the absolute scale of a business in terms of factors such as output and employment.

Business growth is an expansion in the size of a business. This growth can be achieved in several different ways.

Measuring business size

Business managers and governments are interested in measuring business size. Two reasons are:

➤ Managers want to know if their business is growing faster than others in the industry.

➤ Governments want to know if national businesses are becoming larger compared with those of other countries and whether the number of small businesses is increasing.

Methods

Value of output or sales: This calculates the total value of the goods produced or sold by a business during a period of time.

Level of employment: Measuring the total number of employees is a common and easy method, but it is important to measure the number of part-time workers correctly. A business with 10 part-time workers on a 10-hour-per-week contract is clearly not larger than a business with four full-time workers on a 40-hour week. In this example, four part-time workers equal one full-time equivalent employee.

Capital employed: This is the value of the long-term and permanent capital invested in the business – long-term loans plus shareholders' equity.

Market capitalisation: This can only be calculated for public limited companies as they have a quoted share price. It is the total value of all of a company's issued shares at the current share price. It can vary daily.

Market share: This is not an absolute measure of size but is the sales of a business (in a period of time) as a percentage of the total market size it operates in. A business's market share can fall despite an increase in sales, if the value of total market sales is rising at a faster rate.

Limitations of the measures

They can give misleading indications, so it is common to use more than one measure to make comparisons. Problems include:

➤ Sales value: Although useful for making comparisons between firms in the same industry, it is of limited value in making inter-industry comparisons.

➤ Employment: This would make, for example, a nuclear power company – with few employees but huge capital investments – appear quite small.

➤ Capital employed: This would make a labour-intensive industry – such as a postal service – appear quite small compared to the large number of people it employs.

➤ Market capitalisation: This excludes large private limited companies. The values can also change greatly with a stock market boom or slump.

➤ Market share: Although useful for making comparisons between firms in the same industry, it is of no use in making size comparisons between firms in completely different industries.

How businesses grow

Business expansion can take place in two ways. Internal or organic growth is through expanding existing operations and opening new ones. It is relatively slow but easy to manage as management should have time to ensure that finance and other resources are available. External growth is through integration with another business by means of a merger or a takeover (acquisition).

There are four types of integration or external growth:

Horizontal integration: merger or takeover between two businesses in the same industry at the same stage of production. A merger is when the management of two businesses agree to combine them to form a larger one. A takeover is when one business buys out the owners of another.

Vertical backward integration: between two businesses in the same industry at different stages of production. 'Backward' means that a business integrates with one of its supplying businesses.

Vertical forward integration: between two businesses in the same industry at different stages of production. 'Forward' means that a business integrates with one of its customer businesses.

Conglomerate integration: between two businesses in different industries, for example a clothing manufacturer and a cosmetics manufacturer.

Impact of integration on stakeholders

Integration can have significant effects on stakeholder groups and can result in 'stakeholder conflict'. This means some stakeholders will benefit more than others and some, in fact, may lose out.

Integration type	Possible impact on business	Stakeholder impact
Horizontal	• Higher market share • More control over market, e.g. in setting prices • Economies of scale – unit costs might fall • Opportunities for cost cutting, e.g. rationalising production onto one site • Greater bargaining power over suppliers	**Customers:** Prices may reduce because the larger business can reduce unit costs. BUT there is less choice and prices could rise as the business now has more market share or power. **Suppliers:** Can supply higher quantities to the larger business. BUT forced to cut cost of supplies as the larger business puts more pressure on them. **Workers:** More opportunities for promotion within larger business. BUT some jobs lost through rationalisation.
Vertical forward	• Control over next stage of production • Control over marketing strategy, e.g. if manufacturer takes over chain of shops • Producer obtains secure outlet for firm's products	**Customers:** Retailers dedicated to selling just one manufacturer's products. BUT less product choice in the manufacturer's own shops. **Senior managers:** May have problems controlling a business in another sector of industry. BUT for employees, opportunities may exist to gain experience in different part of industry.
Vertical backward	• Control over supplier • Able to monitor quality of supplies more easily • Able to control costs of supplies • Opportunity for combined research into improved materials or components	**Customers:** Product quality may improve as firm has control over suppliers. BUT the business may refuse to supply materials or components to other manufacturers, limiting product choice. **Managers:** May have problems controlling a business in another sector of industry. BUT for employees, opportunities may exist to gain experience in different part of industry.
Conglomerate	• Diversification of risks by moving into different products and markets • These products or markets may offer opportunities for faster growth.	**Managers and workers:** Greater career opportunities. BUT business may lack focus and sense of direction which may reduce motivation. More chance of a clash of cultures between businesses operating in different industries.

The overall benefits of integration depend on the level of synergy that results from the merger or takeover. Reasons for failing to achieve the benefits claimed for it include:

➤ There may be a clash of management styles and cultures between the two businesses.

➤ The motivation of the combined workforce may fall if redundancies are planned.

➤ The problems of managing a much bigger business outweigh the potential cost savings.

➤ Stakeholders become concerned about increased market share and power of the expanded business.

Risks of rapid growth

Businesses sometimes experience serious problems as a result of expanding too quickly:

➤ **Lack of capital:** Additional fixed assets may be needed. The cost of a takeover may be very high. Running short of working capital during rapid expansion is sometimes called 'overtrading'.

➤ **Lack of management expertise:** Rapid growth may put strains on existing managers and new managers may take time to understand how the business operates.

➤ **Marketing and production departments:** Problems include whether there is sufficient capacity to supply many more customers and whether different marketing strategies will be needed.

Case study

In 2011 Microsoft took over Skype and paid $8.5bn to the owners of the Internet telephone service company. Some business analysts believe that the price was too high, but what benefits does Microsoft expect from this integration?

It gains direct access to Skype's 600 million users worldwide which is vertical forward integration. Skype can be operated on all of Microsoft's operating systems, resulting in a potentially huge mobile phone market for international mobile phone calls via Skype. Microsoft can expand Skype into the industrial telephone market, which would be diversification.

If Skype's technology is linked in with Microsoft's Xbox Kinect and an HD TV, Microsoft can gain access to millions of consumers' living rooms and market products such as family teleconferencing, one-to-one tuition and home schooling.

Summary

The size of businesses can be assessed in several ways. Relative size can be measured by market share. Businesses can expand either internally (organically) or externally. External growth is integration through mergers or takeovers and can be achieved in several ways. External growth impacts on different stakeholder groups in different ways. Rapid growth can be risky if not well managed.

Entrepreneurs

Enterprise refers to the actions of a person when showing initiative in setting up a business and taking risks by investing in it and operating it.

Entrepreneurs are the people who show this enterprise – they take advantage of an opportunity to set up and invest in a new business venture and take on the risks associated with it.

What makes an entrepreneur?

An entrepreneur is determined to create their own business, not work for someone else. They must have a business idea, have capital to invest and be willing to take risks and accept responsibilities.

An entrepreneur supplies risk capital as a risk taker, and monitors and controls the business activities. Most regard profit as a standard for measuring their achievement or success.

The key characteristics of a successful entrepreneur are:

Committed and self-motivated: The entrepreneur may have to work many hours with low rewards.

Leadership qualities: If the business employs people, the workers need to share in the entrepreneur's vision.

Risk taking: Investing their own money means that the entrepreneur is risking their job security and their savings if the business fails.

Self-confident: The entrepreneur needs to display confidence in their business idea and their ability to make it succeed.

Innovative: A new business may need to offer a very different product or service to its established competitors.

Multi-skilled: The entrepreneur may need to undertake many different tasks within the business.

Why some new enterprises fail

➤ Lack of finance or working capital

➤ Poor record keeping, such as accounts

➤ Poor management skills

➤ Competition

➤ Changes in the economy or technological developments

Enterprise: benefits for the country

➤ Unemployment may be reduced.

➤ Output will increase.

➤ There will be more competition for existing businesses.

➤ Government tax revenue should increase.

➤ New technology may be developed.

Case study

In four years, Richard Hurtley has gone from selling his own-brand, highly-coloured socks at Exeter University to running a nationwide fashion company, Rampant Sporting, which has 20 employees and two high-street stores.

His determination to succeed was partly due to not finding employment. He invested £2,000 of his own money but has recently obtained other finance from his bank and the fashion chain Joules. The growth in sales of 450% this year is just the start. Richard is even considering expansion abroad.

Summary

Enterprise is important for the establishment of new businesses and for an economy's growth. Entrepreneurs take risks in setting up new businesses, driven by motives other than just profit. Successful entrepreneurs have many important personal qualities and skills.

Legal structure

The legal structure of a business refers to its form of ownership. Private sector businesses can either be incorporated (they have a separate legal identity to the owners of the business) or unincorporated (the business owners and the business are one and the same). There are also businesses owned by the government called public corporations.

Different types of legal structure:

Features	Advantages	Disadvantages
Sole trader One owner – controls the business – keeps the profits. Finance from own savings, bank loan, overdraft. Examples: electrician, hairdresser	• Easy to set up/no formal documentation • Own boss • Owner keeps the profits • Privacy in accounts • Quick to respond to customers needs	• Unlimited liability so owner could lose personal possessions • No one to discuss business issues with • No continuity – if owner dies so does the business • Lack of capital for expansion
Partnership 2–20 partners. May choose to have a Deed Partnership – sets out terms of partnership. Finance – Partners savings, bank loan, overdraft. Example: solicitors	• Partners keep the profits • Privacy in accounts • More capital from partners • Partners can specialise in tasks • Decisions can be made quickly	• Unlimited liability (with some exemptions) • No continuity • Responsible for partners' actions • Limited capital when compared to Ltd or plc
Limited Liability Partnership (LLP after its name). 2 or more members own the business and are paid the profits. Finance – members' savings, bank loan, overdraft Example: accountants	• Limited liability so the owners can only lose the money they invested • Have a simplified form to complete to register with Companies House • No change in tax status if changed from a partnership to a LLP	• Still need to file a tax return with Companies House • Partners/members are still personally responsible if found to give negligent advice to client

Features	Advantages	Disadvantages
Private limited company (Ltd or Pte after its name) Shareholders: 2 or more & controlled by a Board of Directors Finance – shares, debentures, bank loans, overdraft, venture capital Profits – Government as tax, dividends to shareholders, retained in company	• Limited liability means can only lose share capital invested in the company • Raise capital by selling shares • Continuity as shares can be sold or given to next of kin • Founders of business keep control if don't sell more than 50% of shares • Greater status than an unincorporated business	• Only sell shares to family and friends not the public • Legal procedures when setting up – need to draw up a Memorandum of Association and Articles of Association – sent to Companies House when registering the company name • Accounts filed with Companies House
Public limited company (plc or inc after its name) Shareholders: 2 or more and controlled by a Board of Directors Finance – shares, debentures, bank loans, overdraft, venture capital, rights issue Profits – Government as tax, dividends to shareholders, retained in company	• Limited liability • Able to raise large amounts of capital by selling shares to the public, often through the Stock Exchange • Continuity as shares can be sold or given to next of kin • Easier to borrow funds because of higher status	• Accounts must be published annually • Easier to take over • Expensive legal formalities when setting up • Share price fluctuations can affect decision making • Split between ownership (shareholders) and control (directors) – potential clash of objectives
Franchise (plc or Ltd or any other form of business organisation) Franchisor (sells the franchise) Franchisee (buys the franchise) The franchisee pays franchisor for rights to trade under franchise name, use the logo, etc.	• Less likely to fail as established brand name/ image • Easier to raise banks loans • Economies of scale for franchisor • Quicker to expand as franchisee pays for expansion	• Franchisee pays a proportion of profits to franchisor • Large capital sum to buy franchise paid for by franchisee • Local promotions still need to be paid by franchisee

Finance - franchisee payment, bank loans, overdraft	• Franchise will not open another outlet nearby	• No choice of suppliers
	• Franchise supplies all materials	• Have to follow franchise prices and layout of store, etc
Examples: McDonald's, Body Shop	• National advertising paid for by franchisor	

Public corporations are owned and controlled by the government, and are sometimes known as nationalised industries. They tend to be major industries such as telecommunication, energy or transport. Their objectives are different from those of private sector businesses – social objectives, such as communication in remote areas of the country, can be as important as profit. If losses are made they will not be closed down.

Case study

Zenith Bank Nigeria plc, one of the largest commercial banks from Nigeria, is now to be listed to trade its shares on the London Stock Exchange. This will give the public limited company access to one of the largest pools of capital in the world, standing at over $1.8 trillion in 2013.

There are another 97 Sub-Saharan African companies that have taken advantage of the larger capital market available and London is the largest international stock exchange for African companies in the world.

Summary

Businesses can operate with different legal structures. Unincorporated businesses (i.e. not companies) are often small and owners do not have limited liability. Incorporated businesses can grow very large. All owners have limited liability. There is often a split between ownership and control.

Opportunity cost

When making any choice, the alternative options have to be given up. The opportunity cost of the choice which has been made is the benefit of the next best alternative that is given up or foregone.

The basic economic problem is that all resources are scarce; there are insufficient factors of production to supply the needs of everyone in the world.

This is not because there is not enough money to go round. Money is just a way to distribute the goods and services that have been produced and if everyone earned twice as much money, there would not be twice as many goods and services to buy. Prices would rise and you would still only be able to buy the same quantity of goods.

Customers, businesses and government have to make choices all the time. When a choice is made, something else has to be given up. The cost in loss of benefits of what you have given up is opportunity cost.

Case study

The HS2 fast rail link between London and Leeds received government backing in 2013. It is estimated to cost £33bn and should result in new jobs, improved communications and additional capacity on the railways. The opportunity cost of this not going ahead is all the  benefits which have been claimed to come from this link. If HS2 is built then the opportunity cost is what else the government might have spent £33bn on.

Summary

Opportunity cost is the next best alternative foregone. It is the alternative which is given up when choices are being made.

Sectors of activity

Business activity involves coordinating resources to produce goods and services that meet the needs of customers.

Business activity can be divided into three sectors – primary, secondary and tertiary – depending on the exact nature of the activity.

The three sectors

Primary sector
These businesses produce or grow raw materials used by other businesses in the secondary sector. They include:

➤ copper, coal and other extracted and mined products

➤ farmed products such as wheat and coffee beans

➤ forestry and fishing.

The raw materials often have relatively low value and the potential for adding value to them by businesses in this sector is limited. It is only when they are converted into manufactured products that significant value is added. This is a secondary sector activity.

Secondary sector
These businesses purchase raw materials and transform them into manufactured products. The products are either:

➤ semi-finished goods that are sold to other businesses, for example, steel made from coal and iron ore

➤ finished products that can be sold to final consumers, such as food processing firms. Secondary sector businesses can add much value to the original raw materials (see: *Value added*).

Tertiary sector
These businesses provide intangible (not physical) goods to other businesses and final consumers. They include theatres

and banks. Other businesses, such as retailers, can provide tangible (physical) goods to other businesses and final consumers. Some tertiary sector businesses are able to add much value to the products they buy in, such as high-class retailers. Others find it more difficult when the service being provided cannot easily be differentiated, such as cleaning services.

The relative importance of sectors

The relative importance of these sectors to a country's economy varies over time. For much of the 19th century, manufacturing industries (secondary sector) accounted for nearly 50% of UK output and employment. Compare this with more recent figures:

UK data	Primary	Secondary	Tertiary
1950 Employment	7.6%	41.0%	51.4%
2012 Employment	1.5%	15.6%	82.9%
2012 Share of GDP	3.6%	20.1%	76.3%

Reasons for these changes include:

➤ Decline in coal mining, steel production, shipbuilding and other heavy industries. These have lost competitiveness to foreign producers and use of coal is diminishing for environmental reasons.

➤ Loss of competitiveness in manufacturing industries such as domestic electrical goods and mass car production (this is referred to as deindustrialisation). Three main factors have been: slow UK productivity growth; relatively high labour costs; low levels of investment in new machinery and products.

➤ Higher living standards have lead to changes in spending patterns. A much higher proportion of average income is spent on services such as holidays and financial services than in 1950.

➤ Higher demands for improved public services such as education and health have led to the expansion of this important part of the tertiary sector.

Differences between countries

➤ In countries with a low average income, such as Cambodia and Papua New Guinea, agriculture and other primary sector activities account for a very high share of both employment and GDP.

➤ Faster-growing emerging market economies, such as Brazil, India and Thailand, have secondary sectors that are growing rapidly.

➤ In most high income countries, such as the UK and France, the tertiary sector accounts for the highest share of employment and GDP.

Contrast the UK data in the table with that for India:

India data	Primary	Secondary	Tertiary
2012 Employment	60%	17%	23%
2012 Share of GDP	25%	24%	51%

Case study

Lafarge is a construction company that operates in all three sectors of business activity. It extracts the raw materials required; it processes them into building materials; it transports the goods; it offers sales and after-sales services to its customers. The company claims this brings key benefits: it gains the value added at all stages in the chain of production; there is effective control of quality and health and safety standards at all stages of production; and the company can monitor its total impact on the environment.

Summary

Business activity is commonly classified into three sectors: the primary, secondary and tertiary sectors. The relative importance of these sectors changes over time and varies between countries.

Specialisation

Specialisation is the splitting up of the production process into clearly defined tasks. Each employee focuses on one task. It is also referred to as 'division of labour'. The concept of specialisation is at the core of modern economies.

The importance of specialisation

Specialisation includes the practice of businesses, regions of a country and whole countries focusing on 'what they do best'. This might be a particular product, service or industry. With the financial returns gained from selling the products that have been specialised in, other products may be bought that have also been produced by specialised employees, businesses, regions and countries.

The benefits are often explained in terms of comparative advantage. This means that individuals, businesses and countries should specialise in what they do best and trade with other individuals, businesses and countries for products they do not produce, leading to an increase in the total output of goods and services.

Division of labour

Adam Smith first explained the benefits of the division of labour in *The Wealth of Nations* (1776). As workers become more experienced at performing their specialised task, output per worker will increase. Smith stated that the division of labour would **always** increase productivity, which could then result in higher wages for workers, higher profits for employers, and better and cheaper products for customers.

Benefits and limitations

To individual workers

Benefits	Limitations
• Specialise in one task and can take pride in a task done very well • Higher productivity could lead to higher wages • Only one skill to learn	• Work can become monotonous • No pride in being multi-talented and flexible • If task can be undertaken by a machine, the worker's skill becomes redundant

The principle of employee specialisation is recognised by most businesses. However, the need to increase flexibility and adaptability of employees due to markets that have constantly changing needs, means that multi-skilling is becoming more common and can benefit the motivation levels of employees.

To businesses

Increasingly, businesses are outsourcing to specialist firms services such as IT, payroll calculations, accounting and customer service. This allows the business to focus on its core activities.

Benefits	Limitations
• Can focus on one sector or activity • Can become renowned specialists in their field • Can reduce unit costs through being focused on one part of production • Can employ specialist managers and purchase specialist equipment	• Dependent on suppliers for quality and reliability of delivery • Dependent on retailers to stock and sell products • Specialist products may be replaced by new technology

To countries

Countries possess different natural features and resources and these determine the products in which they have a comparative advantage. Total world output will be higher than it would be if every country tried to be self-sufficient.

Benefits	Limitations
• Raises output of products in which country has competitive advantage	• If it specialises in natural resources, these may be over-exploited
• Can trade with other countries that have advantages in other products	• It may be vulnerable to changes in demand or in technology that makes existing products less competitive
• Increases living standards	

Case study

TopCoder is a software development business based in Connecticut which employs very few staff directly. It splits its clients' new IT projects into a large number of small, operations and offers these to its worldwide connections in the IT industry. Some specialist operators will suggest a new software idea, others will develop the system requirement and others will devise the system's architecture. TopCoder will select IT experts to concentrate on the programming and another specialist to integrate the whole system. This method of working allows IT experts from around the world to focus on what they do best.

Summary

Specialisation by workers is also known as division of labour. Focusing on tasks that workers are skilled in should increase productivity. Businesses, regions and countries also specialise and there are benefits and limitations to this.

Value added

Value added is the difference between the selling price of a good or service and the cost of the inputs involved in making it. Most businesses try to maximise 'added value' to the materials they purchase, so that the selling price of the product is greater than the total cost of those materials.

What is added value?

All businesses buy inputs such as materials, components or services from other businesses. If a washing machine manufacturer set its selling price at the same level as the total cost of the inputs of materials and components used, it would not be adding value. It would not be making any profit either!

The same principle applies in service sector businesses such as restaurants. Top class restaurants might charge £40 for one course but the cost of the food content would be much less than this. If the food and other input costs were £10 for this one course, then the restaurant has added value of £30 to the inputs. The name, reputation and image of the restaurant and the quality of the cooking allow the business to add value to the food it buys in by charging a price substantially above cost.

How can value be added?

Value can be added by creating a differentiated product that customers are prepared to pay a higher price for. Increasing the price **without** a strategy to offer a better service, differentiate the product or establish a brand that consumers want to buy in to, will lead to lower sales. These are the most commonly used ways of increasing value added by increasing price:

➤ Developing differentiated products that have an unusual or unique feature

➤ Offering exceptional customer service or customer experience

➤ Effectively branding a product with a name, image and logo that customers want to be associated with – and will pay a premium price to do so.

Value can also be added by cutting input costs but maintaining the selling price. This might be done by sourcing supplies from cheaper producers, perhaps located abroad. The big unknown factor is whether this will reduce the actual or perceived quality of the product. If it does, then the selling price might have to be reduced and added value might not, after all, show any increase. Another method to increase value added by reducing costs is to reduce waste at all stages of the production process – this will then require fewer inputs for the same value of output (see: *Lean production*).

Importance of value added to a business

A business that successfully adds value to its production process should benefit from the following:

➤ Higher prices, without substantially higher costs. This will increase profit margins – and if sales do not fall, higher total profits.

➤ Higher profits allow increased investment in even further improvements to the product and customer service.

➤ Increased differentiation allows market segmentation, reduces the risk of competition, and reduces price elasticity of demand, at least until rivals adopt similar strategies.

Profit (which is revenue minus costs) should not be confused with value added. To arrive at value added, only the cost of bought-in inputs is subtracted from revenue (or selling price if the value added of one unit is being calculated). Value added does not take into account other costs of the business such as employee costs and overheads.

Case study

Times are hard in agriculture. Farmers in the US state of Oregon are being encouraged to raise their incomes by adding value to their crops. Instead of selling them in an unprocessed form to large food-processing businesses at very low prices, schemes have been established for the farmers to gain value added for themselves. Through packaging, processing, drying and other methods, farmers can charge higher prices for their salad crops, fruit and meat products. Increasingly, value added food products grown locally are hitting the local market as farmers take advantage of high demand, low price-elastic niche markets.

Summary

Value added is gained by selling products for more than the cost of inputs. Value added can be increased by charging higher prices or reducing input costs. Higher prices are only likely to be effective if differentiated products and services are developed and if branding is successful.

Communication

Communication is the passing of a message from the sender to the receiver, who understands the message. The message is the information or instructions passed by the sender to the receiver. Internal communication is between members of the same organisation. External communication is between the organisation and other organisations or individuals.

Effective communication

Communication only works well if it is **effective**. This means that the message being sent is received, understood and acted upon in the way intended. Communication failure can have serious consequences, for example:

➤ Employees fail to understand health and safety information.

➤ Managers fail to understand customer feedback on products from employees.

➤ Suppliers fail to understand the exact requirements of an order for materials from a business.

Effective communication involves four features:

Transmitter (sender) of the message. This is the person passing on the information, who must choose how the message is sent and to whom, to make sure the communication is effective.

Medium (method) of communication for sending the message, for example a letter or noticeboard.

Receiver of the information – the person to whom the message is sent.

Feedback – the receiver confirms that the message has been received and responds to it.

Internal and external communication

The main difference between internal and external communication is **who** is being communicated with:

Internal communication is sending messages between employees within an organisation. This can be one-way communication – no feedback is asked for.

Two-way communication is often more effective. This allows (or sometimes requires) the receiver to respond with either an acknowledgement that the message has been received and understood, or a discussion about the points raised. Two-way communication is essential to encourage active participation.

External communication is with external stakeholders such as suppliers, creditors, customers and official bodies such as the tax authorities. The growth of social networking sites has transformed how a business can communicate externally.

Methods of communication

Verbal or oral communication methods include:

➤ video conferencing: groups of people in different locations communicate through a video link

➤ one-to-one talks or meetings

➤ telephone conversations

➤ meetings and team briefings.

Advantages of verbal communication:

➤ Information can be given out quickly and to a large number of people.

➤ There is opportunity for immediate feedback and two-way communication.

➤ Seeing the speaker, their body language and facial expressions, helps to put the message across effectively.

Disadvantages of verbal communication:

➤ In a big meeting, there is no way of telling whether everybody is listening or has understood the message.

➤ Can be time-consuming as discussion, feedback and two-way communication are encouraged.

➤ Does not provide an accurate and permanent record of the message when needed, such as a warning to a worker.

Written methods of communication include:

➤ business letters (used internally or externally)

➤ memos: written messages used only internally

➤ reports: detailed documents about a particular issue, often produced by experts working in the business

➤ notices: displayed on boards and used to display information which is open to everyone

➤ text messages: an easy and discreet way of communicating with others

➤ electronic means (email, social networking sites, tweeting, etc): have revolutionised the ways many businesses communicate with their customers.

Advantages of written communication:

➤ Evidence of the message exists, which can be referred to in the future.

➤ Essential for messages involving complicated details, which might be misunderstood if verbal methods were used.

➤ Messages can be copied and sent to many people.

➤ Electronic communication is a quick, cheap way to reach large numbers of people.

Disadvantages of written communication:

➤ Direct feedback is not always possible, unless electronic communication is used.

➤ Not easy to check that the message has been received and acted upon.

➤ Language used can be difficult and the message too long to retain interest.

➤ No opportunity for body language to reinforce the message.

➤ Feedback is not immediate or necessarily encouraged.

Reducing barriers to communication

Description of barrier	How to overcome the barrier
Caused by the sender	
• Language may be inappropriate and include jargon or technical terms.	• Use language which is understandable and avoid jargon.
• The sender speaks too quickly or not clearly enough.	• Make the message as clear as possible and ask for feedback.
• The message is too long and detailed so the main points are not understood.	• Keep the message as brief and clear as possible.
Caused by the method of communication	
• Wrong method used, e.g. important message put on a noticeboard which most people did not read.	• Select the appropriate media for each message sent.
• Long chain of command could mean message becomes distorted.	• Use the shortest possible channel.
• Breakdown of the medium, e.g. computer failure or postal strike.	• Make sure other forms of communication are available if possible.

Caused by the receiver	
• May not be listening or paying attention.	• Receiver should be asked for feedback to ensure understanding.
• May not like or trust the sender and so be unwilling to act upon message.	• Consider using another sender who is respected by the receiver.
Lack of feedback	
• There is no feedback.	• Receiver to acknowledge receipt of message and understanding.
• Feedback is received too slowly or is distorted.	• Use more direct lines of communication between subordinates and managers.

Case study

Social networking sites, blogs and Twitter have revolutionised the ways in which businesses can communicate with their customers. These media have increased the importance of 'customer relationship marketing', which aims to increase customer loyalty. Here are some examples:

➤ Red Bull has a Twitter stream from sponsored athletes and celebrities on its Facebook fan page.

➤ Dell has several different corporate blogs each focused on specific customer selected topics, and embeds custom-made videos into blog posts.

➤ Whole Food uses Twitter to invite customers to company events whilst actively asking what they like reading, watching and eating.

Summary

Businesses need to communicate internally and externally. Effective communication is not just about sending messages; it involves selecting the right person to send the message, the right person to receive it, the best medium to use and a means of feedback. Information technology is transforming the ways businesses communicate both internally and externally.

Delegation

Delegation is the process of passing on to others the authority to do certain tasks and take decisions. It is a key feature of the development of employees, aiming to show trust in them by giving them more challenging and significant jobs to do. The passing of authority by senior management to subordinates does not mean that the final responsibility for outcomes has been transferred too – this rests with senior management.

Why delegate?

Delegation is based on the idea that the senior management team cannot do everything in a business. They cannot perform all tasks necessary in the business, take all of the decisions needed and respond to all day-to-day problems that arise.

Managers must focus on setting the key strategic direction of the business, so they delegate other tasks to subordinates at all levels of the organisation. Take the case of a large department store:

➤ The Board of Directors decide the overall strategy of the store in terms of target markets being aimed for.

➤ The directors of each department may delegate to each departmental manager the task of deciding which products to buy for their department.

➤ The departmental managers delegate to each section head the decision about how products are displayed.

➤ Section heads delegate to senior sales staff decisions on which products to mark down in a sale and by how much.

➤ Senior sales staff may delegate to shop floor assistants the authority to deal with a customer complaint.

The concept of delegation is closely linked to both non-financial methods of motivation (see: *Non-financial incentives*) and organisation structure (see: *Organisation structure*).

Stages of successful delegation

Effective delegation is not about telling someone to do something. It will only be successful if these key stages are carried out:

1. **Define the task.** It is important that the tasks being delegated are understood so that the delegate does not do more or less than required.

2. **Select the person or team.** This is likely to be the person or team who will undertake the duties most efficiently and gain most from it.

3. **Identify training needs.** If the task is new to the person or team, they may need some training.

4. **Explain the reasons.** The worst reason to give is 'because I'm too busy'. The most motivating reasons are likely to be 'to develop you in the job' or 'because I trust you to do a good job'.

5. **Explain the required outcome.** How will the delegate know whether they have done a good job? How will this be assessed?

Potential advantages

➤ **Managers can focus on top-level tasks.** These include setting the strategic direction of the business.

➤ **Good on-the-job training.** Employees who are delegated tasks will gain useful experience at accepting authority and taking decisions.

➤ **Empowers and develops employees.** By trusting employees to undertake more challenging tasks and take decisions, they become empowered and gain self-esteem, contributing to the success of a business.

➤ **Quicker decisions.** Decisions are likely to be taken more quickly.

➤ **Better decisions.** Allowing junior employees to take decisions on matters they have direct involvement with means the decisions are likely to be more appropriate.

➤ **Reduces management stress.** By delegating to more junior colleagues, senior managers have less stress.

Potential limitations

➤ **Delegating the wrong tasks.** If employees are given tasks just because the manager does not like doing them, bad feelings will develop.

➤ **Not providing necessary training or resources.** If tasks are delegated to people who have not been trained or do not have the necessary resources, the final results are likely to be disappointing.

➤ **Not making the expected outcome clear.** If people are asked to perform tasks with no clear sense of direction or purpose, delegation is unlikely to work effectively.

➤ **Some loss of control.** Delegation involves trusting people but also accepting some loss of control. Sometimes delegation will lead to bad results or poor decisions as a result. This is unlikely to happen if the stages of successful delegation are followed.

Retaining responsibility

Delegating the authority for a decision to another employee does **not** mean delegating the final responsibility for it. If the final outcome is a failure, the manager who delegated the task must take full responsibility for it.

Case study

Chris owns a successful graphic arts business with an annual turnover of £1m. His main problem is that he has not been able to free up enough time to look for new contracts or projects. His work style is to try to do everything himself.

Working with a business consultant, Chris agreed to make key changes to his management approach:

➤ Chris now delegates projects and asks employees for feedback on how they can do more challenging work.

➤ Employees now mostly deal with clients' issues and pass on to Chris only problems that they can't resolve.

Chris now has more time to develop projects to take the business forward.

Summary

Delegation allows senior managers to have time to focus on strategic issues and to develop more junior employees. It involves a loss of control but an increase in trust. Delegation is more likely to be successful if the stages of successful delegation are followed carefully. Responsibility for a task or a decision cannot be delegated.

Employing workers

When recruiting staff, a business must take into account a number of laws which are designed to protect employees. This starts with a legal requirement to offer an employment contract (pay, hours, holiday entitlement) but also covers laws that ensure the health and safety of the employees.

Contract of employment

An employee will sign a contract of employment. This is a legal document, as set out in the Employment Rights Act, 1996, which sets out the terms and conditions of their employment. It includes details such as job title, hours of work, pay, holiday entitlement, and notice of termination of the contract (how much notice either the employee or the employer should give). The Minimum Wage Act, 1998 also protects employees from low rates of pay.

Working hours

Part-time employees work reduced hours (part of the day or week) in comparison with their full-time colleagues. Part-time work can be beneficial to the employer and to the employee too. These employees now have the same employment rights as full-time employees under the Part-time Employees (Prevention of Less Favourable Treatment) Regulations, 2000 and Employment Relations Act, 1999.

Full-time employees cannot be made to work more than 48 hours in a week, as set out in the European Working Time Regulations, 1998. There are exceptions, such as junior hospital doctors. However, employees can choose to work longer than 48 hours. Employees are entitled to a minimum holiday entitlement of 28 days a year.

Flexible working

Some laws facilitate more flexible working. Employees may want the chance to vary when hours are worked. The Employment Act, 2002 grants the right to ask for flexible hours to employees such as parents of children under 16 or disabled children under 18.

Working from home can also aid this flexibility, as employees do not need to travel to work and can start early in the morning or late at night. Another flexible job pattern is job-share, where two people do a job between them.

Health and safety

Employees should expect to be able to go to work and not be injured. The Health and Safety at Work Act, 1974 covers both the employer and the employee, giving responsibility to work safely both for themselves and not to injure others.

Are these laws bad for employers?

Implementing these laws may raise costs, leading to price increases, so the business may be less competitive against foreign businesses where wages are low and there is less employee protection. However, within the same country, all businesses have to offer the same protection to employees, so will not be less competitive.

Tired employees are likely to be less efficient or productive and there may be more accidents, causing stoppages or reduced efficiency if the employee has to be replaced temporarily.

Redundancy and dismissal

A business may need to remove employees, perhaps when it is restructuring or going through falling sales.

Redundancy is when a particular job is no longer needed and so the employee who does that job is no longer required. A business must go through a fair process of deciding which employees need to be made redundant as laid out in the Employment Rights Act, 1996. A period of notice must be given and a redundancy payment made to the employees.

The ACAS code of practice on discipline and grievance says that if an employee has not been performing satisfactorily or their attendance is poor, they must be given verbal and written warnings before they can be dismissed, unless there is gross misconduct.

Dismissal can be lawful if:

➤ the employee gave false information when recruited

➤ they cannot carry out their duties satisfactorily

➤ there is serious misconduct.

Dismissal is unlawful if:

➤ there is discrimination over race, gender, religion or age

➤ the employee becomes pregnant

➤ the employee joins a trade union.

Case study

Managers at Wet Seal Store, USA (a women's clothing store) were said to have only wanted employees who had the 'Armani look': were slim, blonde, and white. The managers said this was necessary to be more profitable. The business was found guilty of race discrimination in 2012.

Summary

Businesses must follow a number of laws to ensure that employees are protected in terms of their health and safety, and in the treatment they receive at work. A contract of employment sets out the terms and conditions of their employment. Employees can expect to be treated fairly and have the right to a hearing if they feel that they have not been treated correctly.

Financial incentives

Financial incentives are different ways of paying employees to reward and motivate them to work effectively for the business. These methods include paying wages and salaries, and additional monetary benefits such as commission, bonuses or profit sharing.

Payment and incentive systems

Managers need to understand the driving forces that motivate workers and use payment methods (financial incentives) that encourage employees to be well motivated.

Payment systems include:

Payment system	Description	Advantages	Disadvantages
Salary, e.g. £30,000 per year for store manager	An amount paid per year usually to non-manual workers	• Security of income • Suitable for jobs where output is not measurable	• No overtime usually paid, so not related to how much effort put in • Quickly loses ability to motivate
Time-rate, e.g. £7.48 per hour for supermarket checkout operator	Workers are paid for each hour they work	• The more hours worked the higher the pay • Used when output is difficult to measure	• Quickly loses ability to motivate • May lead to slow rate of work • May take time to calculate and track hours worked
Piece-rate e.g. £5 per item produced on a production line	Payment based on the amount of output produced. Used when output can be easily measured	• Incentive to work harder to produce more output and receive more pay	• Workers may rush work so quality may fall • May lead to customer complaints and increased costs from returns of faulty goods

Payment system	Description	Advantages	Disadvantages
Fringe benefits, e.g. extra holidays, pension schemes, company car and phone, free private health care, discount on company products	Additional benefits received in addition to wage or salary	• Additional incentives to attract people to become an employee • Some fringe benefits are tax free so it is cheaper than paying higher basic wage/salary for the business	• Soon become expected and lose their effect to motivate workers

Incentive schemes related to performance:

Payment system	Description	Advantages	Disadvantages
Bonus	Sum of money paid in addition to normal payment, based on achieving a performance target	• Encourages employees to work hard to achieve targets set	• Can be difficult to measure which workers have contributed to the achievement of targets
Profit sharing	Percentage of profits made will be paid to employees in addition to normal pay	• Encourages all employees to work hard together to increase profits	• Workers get the same proportion of profit whether they have worked hard or not
Commission	A percentage of sales, often paid in addition to low basic pay	• Incentive to make more sales • Incentive to work harder to receive more pay	• Workers may not consider customer needs as they want to make a sale – leads to unhappy customers • Stressful for sales staff if having a bad month/week in terms of sales made

Payment system	Description	Advantages	Disadvantages
Share ownership	Employees are given the option to buy a set number of shares in the future at current share price	• Encourages workers to work hard for the success of the business to increase share price/profits • Used when difficult to identify/ measure individual performance of workers • May improve employee loyalty	• Share prices can increase/decrease due to other factors, e.g. in a recession • Paid no matter how much effort is put in

Value of a well-motivated workforce

➤ Higher production or output because productivity is higher and unit costs are reduced.

➤ Lower staff turnover, which reduces recruitment and training costs.

➤ Higher staff morale, leading to a better working environment.

➤ Lower absenteeism because workers are happier and less likely to take time off unless absolutely necessary.

➤ High quality work produced with fewer mistakes so fewer customer complaints.

➤ More innovative ideas put forward by workers who feel part of the business and want to improve the product or service.

➤ Good reputation as an employer helps attract skilled workers.

Remember that financial motivation methods cost the business money, so the increases in output or efficiency must more than make up for this cost.

Case study

John Lewis Partnership pay 'partners' (their workers) according to the market rate for the job they are doing, and more if they exceed expectations. Each partner is paid an annual bonus which is a proportion of profits as a percentage of salary. The John Lewis Partnership offers a non-contributory, final salary pension scheme after three years' service. After three months' service, all partners are entitled to discount on most purchases from John Lewis and Waitrose. Subsidised dining facilities offer good food at reasonable prices.

Summary

Financial methods can increase motivation. They include increased payment for increased output, and increased sales to reward the worker for a good job carried out. Having well-motivated workers is hugely beneficial in terms of increasing productivity and reducing unit costs for the business.

Leadership

Leadership is the skill of motivating and inspiring a group of people towards achieving a common objective.

Management and leadership are very closely linked but there are significant differences. They are both focused on achieving an organisation's objectives. Management is about getting things done by organising and controlling resources. Leadership involves making people committed to want to achieve the objectives.

Leadership skills

Not everyone can become an effective leader. Successful leaders often have all or most of the following personal qualities:

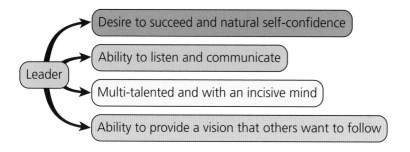

Leaders need to be able to inspire others. They should provide a long-term vision that people can understand and relate to. They set long-range goals. They must then provide strategic direction, outlining their vision and objectives. The best leaders provide purpose and meaning, building communities by creating a sense of trust, confidence and belief, inspiring people to follow them, and challenging followers to become the best they can be.

Importance of leadership

Employees expect the following from their leaders:

➤ a clear vision for the business and a sense of direction

➤ confident and effective decision making

➤ accurate planning

➤ ability to lead a business through difficult times or periods of great change

➤ support and commitment for employee welfare.

Styles of leadership

There are several different leadership styles. No one style is best for all business situations.

Autocratic: The leader takes all decisions, supervises employees closely and only provides one-way communication.

Democratic: This leader encourages employee participation in decision making. Two-way communication is used to allow for feedback. The staff involvement can be motivating.

Paternalistic: These leaders do what they think best for workers. There may be some consultation but the leader always takes final decisions.

Laissez-faire: Managers delegate virtually all authority and decisions.

Bureaucratic: Clearly defined rules are followed in all situations. Decision making is centralised.

Here are the possible advantages and limitations of each style:

Style	Advantages and application	Limitations
Autocratic	• Allows rapid, consistent decision making. • Used in armed forces, police, etc when a crisis occurs	• Demotivating for employees as no involvement in decision making • Management decision making does not benefit from employees' experience and ideas
Democratic	• Allows employee involvement in decision making • Used in organisations that value employees' contribution, adding to the success of decision making	• Consultation and involvement can be time consuming • Some issues might be too complex or sensitive for employees to be involved, e.g. redundancies, complex technical issues
Paternalistic	• Allows for employee ideas to be discussed and for employee welfare to be considered • Used by organisations with strong leaders but who value employee ideas	• Having some involvement in discussing business issues – but not in the final decision – might lead to employee frustration • Workers may resent the 'we know what is good for you' focus
Laissez-faire	• Allows employees considerable influence in controlling their own work practices and deciding how goals should be achieved • Used in research and creative-based organisations where employees respond to trust and freedom	• Lack of management supervision may not always be appropriate • If managers are just weak and allow employees independence this is unlikely to lead to success
Bureaucratic	• Allows workers to operate within tightly-controlled limits according to their job description • Used in organisations where consistent application of rules and regulations might be essential	• Not motivating to employees if they are searching for challenging jobs offering participation and independence • Discourages employees from thinking for themselves to solve problems

Choice of leadership style

The most effective leadership style depends on the following factors:

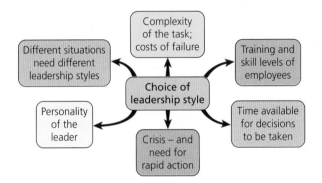

Informal leadership

Formal leaders, with formal authority over subordinates, are appointed by the business. Informal leaders are people who have no formal authority but have influence over others in the organisation. Often this influence stems from great experience or a forceful personality. Organisations often try to identify these informal leaders and encourage them to influence other employees, for example, to accept a significant change that is being planned.

Case study

Over the past five years Jim Sinegal has led his company Costco to impressive returns. The share price has doubled, and revenue continues to grow at an impressive rate. Yet Sinegal might be better known as a man of the people at Costco. His name tag says 'Jim', he answers his own phone, and his plain office at the company headquarters doesn't even have walls.

While other CEOs are spending tens of thousands of dollars decorating their offices, Sinegal pays himself a yearly salary of $350,000. Most CEOs of large companies are paid in the millions. He believes he shouldn't be paid more than 12 people working on the floor. His simple contract is only a page long, and even includes a section that outlines how he can be dismissed for not doing his work. Costco's employee turnover rate is the lowest in the retail industry, over five times less than rival Wal-Mart. In an age where CEOs would never be seen 'as one of the employees', Jim Sinegal is unusual – and his employees respect him for it.

Summary

Leadership is shown when people can inspire and motivate employees. Certain personal qualities and skills are needed to become an effective leader. There are several different leadership styles. No single leadership style is appropriate at all times.

Management

Management is the organisation and coordination of business activities to achieve defined objectives. All businesses need management in some form. Even a sole trader with no employees must carry out management tasks such as making decisions about the allocation of resources and the planning of activities.

The functions of management

Managers of a business perform many functions:

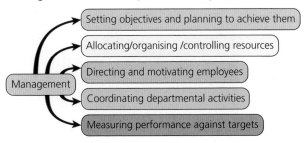

Setting objectives: See: *Business objectives.*

Allocating, organising and controlling resources: Management must decide how best to allocate limited resources to departments. These must be spent effectively and the performance of the assets purchased should be controlled.

Directing and motivating employees: This is a key management function in any business. The methods used to direct and motivate will vary depending on various factors (see: *Leadership*).

Coordinating departmental activities: In a traditional hierarchical organisation, departments can become too 'blinkered'. Senior management should ensure that the objectives of all departments remain focused on the overall aims of the business.

Measuring performance against targets: It is management's responsibility to achieve the organisation's objectives, and to frequently measure the performance of its activities against the targets.

Management roles

Managers have to undertake many roles. Henry Mintzberg, a writer on management theories, groups managerial roles and activities in the following way:

Category	Role	Activity
Informational	Monitor	Seek and receive information, scan papers and reports, maintain interpersonal contacts
	Disseminator	Forward information to others, send memos, make phone calls
	Spokesperson	Represent the unit to outsiders in speeches and reports
Interpersonal	Figurehead	Perform ceremonial and symbolic duties, receive visitors
	Leader	Direct and motivate subordinates, train, advise and influence
	Liason	Maintain information links in and beyond the organisation
Decisional	Entrepeneur	Initiate new projects, spot opportunities, identify areas of business development
	Disturbance handler	Take corrective action during crises, resolve conflicts amongst staff, adapt to external changes
	Resource allocator	Decide who gets resources, schedule, budget, set priorities
	Negotiator	Represent department during negotiations with unions, suppliers, and generally defend interests

Management skills

Managers need important skills to perform these roles. Some skills can be taught and will develop with experience:

➤ **Communication:** Effective two-way communication should lead to good feedback from employees.

➤ **Decision making:** Quick decision making, weighing up options and analysing advantages and disadvantages can be essential for success.

➤ **Problem solving:** Analysing a short-term crisis situation or a long-term underlying problem should increase the chances of a good solution.

➤ **Time management:** Delegating to others is essential to allow more time to be spent on really important long-term and strategic issues.

➤ **Conflict management:** Resolving disputes between departmental managers is important to ensure a positive and well-focused group of managers.

➤ **Team building:** Managers need to be good team builders and leaders.

Case study

According to a recent survey by Google, having 'a terrible boss' is the most important reason why people leave a company. Managers have a much greater impact on employees' performance and how they feel about their job than any other factor.

Summary

Management is about achieving objectives by organising and controlling other people and resources effectively. Managers perform many functions and roles. Successful managers need certain inter-personal and other skills.

Measuring performance

Employee performance is about how effectively employees are undertaking their job related tasks. There are many ways of measuring and evaluating this performance. The choice of the most effective ones to use depends on the type of business and the nature of its products. Appraisal is the assessment of an employee's performance against pre-set criteria.

Measures of performance

Good workforce performance can be very beneficial to a business. It is important to be able to measure it and take steps to improve it if necessary. These are the most common quantitative measures of employee performance:

$$\text{Labour productivity} = \frac{\text{total output in time period}}{\text{total employees}}$$

$$\text{Absenteeism} = \frac{\text{total days lost by absenteeism}}{\text{total days that could have been worked}} \times 100$$

$$\text{Labour turnover} = \frac{\text{no. of employees leaving per year}}{\text{total employees}} \times 100$$

Product rejection and wastage rates

Customer feedback and complaints rates

Days lost through strikes

Labour productivity (see: *Production and productivity*): High productivity helps improve the efficiency of a business. In some industries it is possible to calculate the output per employee, but this is not always easy. More qualitative performance measures are needed.

Absenteeism: If this is high, it often reflects a poorly-motivated workforce.

Labour turnover: This is both a measure of how committed workers are to an organisation and a reflection on the business's recruitment and selection methods.

Potential benefits of high labour turnover:

➤ New ideas constantly being brought into the business

➤ Low average age of employees is likely – might be more adaptable to technology developments

➤ May reduce labour costs, without the need for redundancies during a recession.

Disadvantages of high labour turnover:

➤ Lack of experienced employees

➤ High recruitment and training costs

➤ Disruptions in production or poor customer service

➤ Reduces morale of employees who remain.

Product returns and wastage rates: Low quality work, possibly a result of poorly-motivated employees, leads to negative customer response.

Customer complaints rates: Productivity is not easy to calculate in some industries so the quality of customer service is a major form of measuring employee performance.

Days lost through strikes: Industrial disputes lead to lost output and poor customer service. A bad strike record could indicate that employees do not share managers' objectives, and that management cannot lead and motivate employees.

Appraising performance

Most organisations appraise (assess) each employee's performance on a regular basis, usually once a year. The most common ways of doing this are:

➤ **Critical incident:** The manager writes down and discusses with the employee the positive and negative performance behaviour of the employee over the performance period.

➤ **Paired comparison analysis:** The manager compares the performance of each employee against each of the other employees.

➤ **Essay appraisal:** The manager and supervisors describe, in writing, the strengths and weaknesses of an employee's behaviour. This non-quantitative appraisal technique may become biased by the writers' views.

➤ **Management by Objectives (MBO):** The manager and employee set objectives for the employee. At the end of the year, they discuss and evaluate the employee's performance against these targets.

Improving employee performance

Performance appraisal: This can be a motivating process as well as a method of evaluating performance. Employees will respond positively to setting their own goals in discussion with their manager.

Training: This can be used to stretch workers, giving them greater flexibility in their work and increasing status and self-esteem.

Cell production or team work: Changing the way in which work is organised can lead to multi-skilling and positive team spirit.

Financial incentives (e.g. profit sharing or share allocation schemes, see: *Financial incentives*)**:** If managed well, these schemes can give employees a stake in the business and encourage greater effort and commitment.

Case study

Nick's Pizza and Pub is a restaurant that has improved employee performance. Many catering businesses have a labour turnover of 200% per year but Nick's is 20%. Customer service ratings and product quality frequently rank in the highest group in the region. Nick has achieved these high levels of employee performance in three ways:

➤ **Encourage employees to ask why** something should be done a certain way and not just how.

➤ **Reward employee training and development**. Annual pay rises are given to those who complete courses successfully and different coloured hats indicate the highest achievers.

➤ **Encourage feedback** from employees, respect their ideas and opinions and act upon them.

Above all Nick believes in: 'treating employees like the creative, intelligent people they are and appraise performance constantly to give immediate feedback to them'.

Summary

Employee performance can be evaluated in several ways. Poor employee performance can have a negative impact on business success. Appraising performance is an important first step towards improving performance. Businesses use various methods to improve employee performance.

Motivation theories

Motivation is the incentive that makes workers want to see a job done efficiently and to the best of their ability. It is created by internal and external factors. Motivation theories analyse and try to understand what motivates workers to want to work. The results of this theoretical work can then be used practically by business managers to decide which motivational incentives – financial and non-financial – should be adopted.

Frederick Taylor (Scientific Management)

Taylor's ideas were developed from studying workers in manufacturing industries and were based on the assumption that all workers are motivated by personal gain: if you pay someone more money, they will work harder.

➤ Jobs were broken down into simple processes and each process timed to see how much output a worker should achieve in a day. If the target output was achieved, they would be paid more money.

➤ Employees were seen like machines. When they were working hard, their productivity would be high so their labour costs would be low.

➤ Workers were treated like any other factor of production and given strict orders.

The theory did not account for the fact that workers are motivated by more than just money. However, it did give rise to large increases in labour productivity in some industries. For many jobs, such as nursing, this is not practical.

Elton Mayo (Human Relations Theory)

This is sometimes called behavioural management. Mayo studied the link between productivity and working conditions at the Hawthorne Works of the General Electric Company, Chicago, focusing on production workers.

➤ The rest periods, work hours, temperature and humidity were varied to see what effect this had on productivity.

➤ He found that it didn't matter if there were changes in working conditions as the workers who were the control group (not affected by the changes) increased their productivity as well as those with better conditions.

➤ He found that it was social interaction which proved to be the most motivating factor for these workers.

➤ He saw work as a social activity and workers responded to having a sense of belonging, recognition and security more than to having a good environment in which to work.

His ideas led to behavioural management techniques to manage the way workers behave towards one another.

Abraham Maslow (Hierarchy of Needs)

Self-fulfilment/Self-actualisation – feels goals have been achieved — e.g. freedom to work at what interests the person

Self-esteem – feels recognised for efforts — e.g. a job title that recognises importance, or pay that indicates status

Social needs – feels a sense of belonging and supported at work/ likes working with others — e.g. working in a team, or being part of a sporting team

Safety needs – feels secure in the job — e.g. health and safety equipment provided, or permanent not temporary contract

Physiological needs – basic needs met for food, water, shelter — e.g. to ensure food and other basic needs can be afforded

➤ Maslow suggested that until certain needs are met an employee cannot be motivated by the next level.

➤ This has implications for the way workers are managed. Managers must identify the level of the hierarchy that a particular job provides and then look for ways of allowing the employees to benefit from the next level up the hierarchy.

Frederick Herzberg (Two-Factor Theory)

Herzberg's motivation theories were based on a study of engineers and accountants. He suggested that humans have two sets of needs:

➤ Hygiene factors are necessary to make a job acceptable and if any of these factors are missing then the worker will feel demotivated.

➤ Motivating factors are those which allow a human being to grow psychologically and feel that their job is worthwhile.

Motivators
Sense of achievement; recognition of effort; personal growth/ development; chance for promotion; nature of the work itself; responsibility
Hygiene factors
Security; working conditions; company policies and administration; relationship with supervisor/line manager; relationship with subordinates; pay/salary

Linking theories and incentives

Taylor: Money is the main motivator. Where output cannot be easily measured, motivators would be performance-related pay, bonus and commission.

Mayo: Non-financial methods are more effective, for example schemes which improve the social environment and praise for a job well done.

Maslow: A combination of financial and non-financial methods is the key.

Herzberg: Financial incentives provide the 'hygiene' factors but non-financial motivation methods are what motivate workers.

Case study

Kellogg's is the world's leading producer of breakfast cereals. The company prides itself on being a great place to work.

Maslow's theory applies in that workers have good rates of pay to provide for their basic living needs. Workers can take career breaks or work from home for a healthy work–life balance. Social needs are met through weekly meetings and workers can contribute ideas as to how the business can be improved. Workers are encouraged to take on challenges and responsibility so they feel fulfilled in their jobs.

The work of Mayo and Herzberg is evident because Kellogg's gives praise and recognition for a job well done.

This approach leads to highly-motivated workers who achieve high levels of productivity, and quality products, resulting in lower unit costs and higher profits.

Summary

There are several different theories about how best to motivate employees. People are a business's most important factor of production and if they are not working efficiently, the business will not compete in the global economy. A business will not be successful with unmotivated workers. The lack of motivators is often a reason why employees leave a job.

Non-financial incentives

Non-financial incentives are forms of reward or improved working methods for employees that do not involve money. They often involve redesigning the job an employee is doing or the methods used, in order to make work more satisfying.

Principles of non-financial incentives

Financial incentives have not always proved effective in achieving improved motivation and productivity. However, the human relations approach to motivation has become more popular with many businesses today. The main principle behind non-financial incentives is that work should have meaning, giving the worker a sense of achievement when the job is completed.

Examples of non-financial incentives include:

➤ Employee takes responsibility for the work done and is trusted to carry it out correctly.

➤ A variety of tasks is built into each job to make work more interesting.

➤ Employee is given influence over how the job is carried out.

➤ Jobs are redesigned to allow for team work and social interaction with other employees.

Types of non-financial motivation

Changing the job design to make work more interesting

➤ **Job rotation** allows workers to switch jobs.

➤ **Job enlargement** is where more tasks of a similar nature are added to the worker's current job.

➤ **Job enrichment** is adding greater responsibility and accountability to a worker's job. This should give workers a challenge and help to develop their unused skills.

➤ **Job redesign** is usually carried out jointly with the employees themselves and is similar to job enrichment.

Job rotation and job enlargement are horizontal extensions to the job (adding tasks which are at a similar level to the current job) but job enrichment and job redesign are vertical extensions to the job (leading to higher levels of responsibility).

➤ **Team working** is changing the arrangement of jobs so that employees work in teams. The skills of the team are shared and the team is responsible for solving any problems. The feeling of belonging makes the team more productive and less likely to be absent.

Involving employees in decision making

➤ **Quality circles** (see: *Quality and customer service*) allow workers not only to contribute to ensuring quality is maintained but also to recommend other improvements. These suggestions will be passed to senior management and may be implemented. Workers who have experience of the actual production process are often much better placed to suggest ways to improve the product or service.

➤ **Worker participation schemes** actively encourage workers to become involved in decision-making within the business. Not only do workers feel valued and part of the organisation, but better decisions may be made as a result of their input.

Goal setting and Management by Objectives (MBO)

Goals or targets are set by the employee and the manager and the employee's performance is measured against those targets. This can be motivating for the employee and beneficial for the business.

Case study

Tesco has won an award for being Britain's top employer in 2013. This was awarded after research by the Corporate Research Foundation Institute into its employee benefits, training schemes and opportunities for career development.

Tesco emphasises self-respect and respect for others and gives praise for hard work. Its 360 degree appraisal system means that the appraisee receives feedback on skills, abilities and behaviour. The contributions of all individuals are recognised and celebrated.

Team working is encouraged and this is part of the company's 'Steering Wheel' strategy, which assesses group and individual work so that staff can work as a team. Employees are valued and recognised as being a vital part of its success.

Summary

Non-financial incentives are designed to improve employee motivation. The methods look at the actual job and ways to make it more interesting. The methods include changing the nature of the job itself or changing the way the employee is managed to encourage participation.

Organisation structure

Organisation structure shows the levels of hierarchy in a business (or any organisation) and the chain of command between the levels.

The structure can be shown on an organisation chart. This shows the levels of hierarchy, the spans of control and the chain of command.

Hierarchical organisation

This is a simple organisational structure:

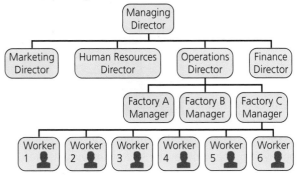

The chart is only complete for Factory C in the Operations Department.

It has the following features:

➤ It is **hierarchical**. Power is greatest at the top and each level has a subordinate apart from the bottom level.

➤ There are four **levels of hierarchy**. Each level has managers or employees of equal authority and status.

➤ The **span of control** of the Managing Director is four. This means that the MD has four people directly reporting to and accountable to him/her.

➤ The **chain of command** runs straight from the top to the bottom. This is the line of authority through which orders and downward communication are passed.

Advantages of a hierarchical organisation
It shows:

➤ the lines of authority

➤ the formal lines of communication between managers

➤ how many people each manager is responsible for

➤ where each individual is in the chain of command and the status of the post they hold

➤ the departmental structure of the business.

Disadvantages of a hierarchical organisation

➤ It can make the organisation inflexible and slow to respond to changes such as consumer tastes or market conditions.

➤ Communication between top and bottom levels of hierarchy can be slow.

➤ Separate departments can lead to poor coordination between them and decisions made can be for the benefit of the department not the whole business.

Tall or short organisation structure?

Compare the following two organisation structures:

Structure A

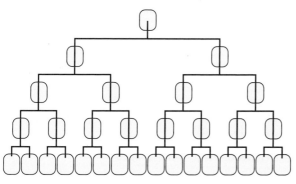

Structure B

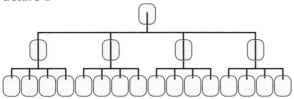

Structure A shows a tall organisation hierarchy. It has many levels of hierarchy and management. This gives it a long chain of command from the top to the bottom of the organisation. Each manager has a narrow span of control.

Structure B shows a wide or flat organisation hierarchy. It has few levels of hierarchy and management. It has a short chain of command. Each manager has a wider span of control than in Structure A.

Most organisations have moved towards a wider, flatter structure by delayering (removing layers of middle management). The potential advantages are:

➤ There are fewer managers, so fixed costs of salaries and other employment-related costs are reduced.

➤ There is a shorter chain of command. This could lead to quicker and more precise communication between top levels and lower levels in the organisation.

➤ There are wider spans of control. Each manager will need to delegate more, which could result in higher levels of motivation for subordinate employees.

The potential disadvantages of delayering are:

➤ There are greater work loads and higher stress levels for each member of staff.

➤ Subordinate staff will need additional training to take on more tasks and this will add to costs.

➤ Fewer management posts mean fewer opportunities for promotion.

Matrix structure – an alternative

An alternative to the hierarchical organisation is called a matrix structure. Teams are established by the allocation of employees from departments of the business. These teams could be given responsibility for particular products or new projects in the business.

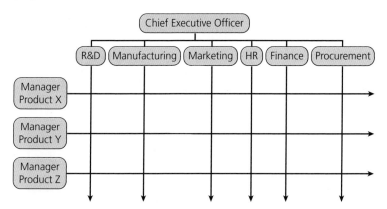

Benefits of matrix structures:

➤ Better communication between departments

➤ Less focus on a vertical chain of command

➤ Greater flexibility – additional project or product teams can be created, or existing ones broken up.

Limitations of matrix structures:

➤ Divided loyalties: Should a worker be more loyal to the department or the product team?

➤ Dual command structure: Which orders or instructions are more important?

➤ Balance of power: Does real authority lie with the department heads or the product team managers?

➤ Much time has to be made available for meetings of all members of the team – and also for departmental meetings.

Case study

Many airlines such as Cathay Pacific have restructured their organisations in recent years by delayering and combining responsibilities between fewer managers. One reason for this has been the increased competition in the industry and the need to cut costs and be able to communicate quickly with junior employees who have direct contact with customers.

Summary

Organisation charts are used to represent lines of authority within an organisation. Traditional hierarchical structures are divided into departments or divisions. The chain of command shows the route taken by authority within such a structure. Spans of control are the numbers of people reporting to each manager. Matrix structures are more flexible than hierarchical structures but can create divided loyalties.

Recruitment

Recruitment is the process of finding and hiring the best-qualified person to fill a job vacancy. Selection is the process of choosing from the applicants a suitable candidate to fill a vacancy.

When is recruitment and selection needed?

➤ **A job becomes vacant**: This might be due to promotion, retirement, dismissal, or because the employee is leaving for a new job.

➤ **A new job has been created**: This might be due to the business being a new start-up, or expanding.

➤ **A new type of job is created, requiring new skills**: Businesses may diversify in their products or services or take over a new company, creating a need for employees with new skills.

Methods of recruitment and selection

The methods of recruitment and selection used will depend on the type of employee being recruited and the reason for the vacancy. The following recruitment process is likely to be followed:

Internal recruitment occurs when applicants already work for the business. Large businesses may offer employees the chance of promotion within the existing business.

External recruitment occurs when applicants work for other businesses and the employees are recruited from outside of the business. This method is used by large and small businesses.

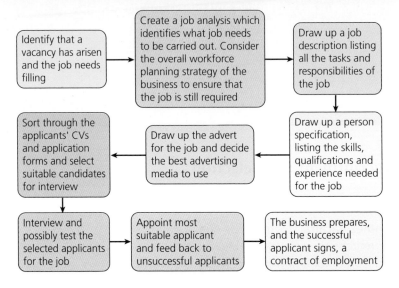

Sometimes, for highly-skilled jobs, the applicant might be approached by the business – they are said to be 'head hunted'. This will be when a particular skill or experience is needed for a job. The business will not advertise the job but instead offer the job to this particular person.

When the business is deciding the recruitment and selection process, it needs to consider the following points:

➤ How big is the business – large or small?

➤ What is the skill mix of current employees?

➤ How skilled does the employee have to be?

➤ Are there skills shortages for this type of job?

➤ What is the recruitment budget?

Selection process

After the business has received either CVs, letters of application and/or application forms, the Human Resources department will draw up a shortlist of suitable applicants. Usually references will be asked for.

Interviewing the shortlisted applicants can take the form of one-to-one, group or panel interviews, where a number of people interview the applicant. Interviews are used to question the applicant about their skills, experience, personality and potential to do the job, and to find out if they will fit with the business ethos.

Selection tests can include aptitude tests. An aptitude test ensures an applicant has the skills to carry out the job. A psychometric test identifies the personality, attitudes and character of the applicant.

Case study

Belfast City Council uses a range of selection processes to select the most appropriate candidate for a job. These include:

Panel short list: A shortlisting panel meets to review the job criteria and match this with the information in application forms.

Testing and assessment: Shortlisted applicants take part in a skills test to assess skills needed for the job.

Interview: If successful at the previous two stages, the applicant attends a structured panel interview with three council officers.

Appointment process: The successful applicant will be asked to:

➤ provide two references

➤ undergo a medical assessment

➤ produce original copies of their qualifications, birth certificate and national insurance number.

Summary

There are several reasons why a business may need to recruit new employees. The recruitment process can either be internal or external. It involves attracting suitable people to apply for the job. The business uses a selection process to find the best person.

Training employees

Training is investment in the human resources of a business. It involves making sure that job holders have the right skills, knowledge and attitudes required to help the business to achieve its objectives. There are three main types of training: induction training, on-the-job training and off-the-job training.

Importance of training

➤ Training helps employees to carry out their job competently and improve their productivity.

➤ By becoming more competent, employees should be happier and less likely to leave.

➤ Training can help employees to do a variety of different jobs. This makes them more flexible.

➤ Training makes it easier to promote employees internally rather than recruit from outside the business.

Types of training

Type of training	Advantages	Disadvantages
Induction training This is training given to new employees, usually by the Human Resources department, when they join the business. It introduces new employees to the business.	The new employee will: • know the layout of the premises • know the health and safety procedures so they stay safe at work • have had a chance to meet new colleagues and so feel more welcome • have been given relevant background information such as a brief history so they feel part of the business.	• It takes time to arrange. • It increases the costs of the HR department. • Output is lost whilst the new employee is having induction training.

Type of training	Advantages	Disadvantages
On-the-job training Employees are shown details of what they have to do. This type of training would be ideal for low-skilled jobs, such as waiters or some administration jobs.	• It is a cheap method of training as no transport costs are required. • The employee can be trained by an existing employee instead of by paid experts. • The employee can practise their job straight away under the supervision of an experienced employee. • The training is very specific to the job. • The employee starts quickly to be productive.	• Any bad habits of the trainer can be passed on to the trainee. • Output is slowed or lost while the training is taking place. • Quality of output of the new employee may be low, which can be expensive to the business.
Off-the-job training The employee is trained away from the place of work. This is often at specialist centres or colleges and is carried out by experts.	• It develops the employee's ability to do their job. • Specialists or experts are used so training is high quality. • Used for existing employees who need a new skill to be developed. • It increases the efficiency of the employee. • It increases promotion prospects for the employee.	• The training may include generic or general skills that are not specific to the job requirements and so wastes time and costs for the business. • The employee may leave and work for another business and so the costs of training will be lost for the business.

Reasons for training

➤ New employees will need induction training.

➤ New jobs have been created by the business and so new skills are needed.

➤ New equipment has been installed and the employees need to know how to operate it.

➤ Employees need to be kept up-to-date, such as a solicitor needing to know about new laws.

➤ Multi-skilling means that an employee can be more flexible in the business and cover for absent colleagues.

➤ Employees will feel more valued if they are offered training to make sure they can do their job effectively.

➤ Training employees so that they gain the necessary skills for promotion can also be motivating.

Case study

Volkswagen has a training academy in Pune, India, for its apprentices and employees. The company wants to provide excellent vocational training and professional development for its employees. The production plant, which was opened in 2009, needs well-trained employees to produce vehicles of a high standard and allow for expansion of production. The academy has the facilities to provide practical training in advanced vehicle and production technologies.

Summary

Training ensures that employees have the right skills, knowledge and attitudes to help a business achieve its objectives. It improves employees' motivation and enables them to be more productive and efficient when carrying out their jobs.

Boston Matrix

The Boston Matrix allows a business to assess its product portfolio at any given time against the rest of the market in which its products are sold. It analyses the share of the market a product has and the rate at which the market is growing. It identifies which products to keep and which products may need to be withdrawn. Other marketing decisions might also be based on this analysis.

What is a Boston Matrix?

A business needs to have a variety of products in its portfolio, including new products if the market is growing, as well as established brands with high market share. Those with low market growth and low market share may need to be withdrawn.

A Boston Matrix is usually drawn like this:

	High market share	Low market share
High market growth	Stars	Question marks or problem children
Low market growth	Cash cow	Dogs

Cash cows have a good brand image and high market share. Sales increase slowly or not at all. The product has brand loyal customers so less marketing is needed and the profit can be used to support other products.

Dogs have low market share and low market growth. Production of these should be stopped.

Question marks or problem children Many new products have low market share. In a rapidly growing market, it is hoped the sales will grow to become cash cows but this may not happen and instead they become 'problem children'. The low market share means it is unlikely to be profitable initially and may need significant marketing expenditure to increase sales.

Stars arise when question marks turn out to have high growth in a growing market. Businesses hope that a 'star' will remain so as long as possible but it may turn into a 'cash cow' or even become a 'dog' instead. Stars are likely to be profitable but the business will need to invest for the growing market.

Using a Boston Matrix

A business will use a Boston Matrix:

➤ To monitor its range of products on a regular basis to see if it needs to develop new products and/or stop producing existing products

➤ To see if new products are turning into stars or cash cows

➤ To assess whether the revenue brought in by cash cows is sufficient to be used to develop new products

➤ To review the continued production of declining products (dogs).

Star	A business may differentiate the product slightly to keep customers interested, e.g. the iPhone keeps having slight changes made.
Dog	Should the business get rid of the product, change its looks or target market, or try to move it out of being a dog? Should the dog be retained if it is still profitable?
Cash cow	These have mainly repeat sales so the business should stimulate sales and remind the target market of the product's existence, e.g. by promotional deals.
Question mark or problem child	The business will need to assess sales and carry out research to see if the product is meeting its objectives, and review the marketing strategy to see if it is appropriate and still effective. Is it worth investing in the new product or is it costing too much relative to sales returns?

Limitations of the Boston Matrix

➤ The business may focus too much on trying to increase the market share of its products when it would be better to try to improve other aspects of the products.

➤ Products produced by the business may be used to support each other. This is why dogs may be kept instead of divesting them.

➤ A dog may still be profitable and provide a positive, even if small, contribution to cash flow for the business.

➤ A star might be sold in a very competitive market and therefore only generate low profit, low profit margin or (occasionally) both.

Case study

The Coca-Cola Company was founded in 1892. Regular Coca-Cola is a cash cow for the company as it has high market share and high sales, but the market is not now growing.

When the company introduced Coca-Cola Light it was a problem child. This product became a star with a high market share and high growth in female market segments. The company then introduced Coca-Cola Zero which it marketed at males. This product is still a question mark. However, its market share is growing and it may become a star. When Cherry Cola was introduced, it started as a question mark but became a dog with low growth and low market share as it was not popular.

Summary

The Boston Matrix is a useful tool to help a business analyse its product portfolio. It helps the business to monitor and review its products and make decisions about whether to continue producing them.

Marketing plans

Marketing is about the different ways a business can seek to both keep its existing customers and add new ones. A marketing plan is a detailed report which sets out the marketing objectives for a product and includes the marketing strategy. A marketing strategy outlines the 4 Ps (Product, Price, Promotion and Place) and how they will combine together to achieve the marketing objectives and so maximise profit.

Marketing objectives

These include:

➤ **Increasing market penetration**, for example Asda trying to gain market share against Tesco

➤ **Increasing market development** by creating new markets, such as clothing retailers having an online presence

➤ **Maintaining market share** and sales and keeping brand loyalty products in the maturity stage of the product life cycle

➤ **Diversifying,** by developing new products for new markets

➤ **Product innovation**, where businesses research and develop genuinely new products.

These marketing objectives can be subject to internal influences such as the finance available, overall corporate objectives of the business or operational issues relating to the way the business is run.

Marketing objectives are also influenced by external influences, which are known as PESTEL factors.

Marketing plan

The structure of a typical marketing plan will be:

➤ **The marketing objectives:** These should be specific, measurable and time limited, for example to increase market share by 3% by the end of next year. (See: *SWOT analysis*.)

➤ **The marketing strategy:** The broad strategy a business will take, such as whether to try to extend sales in the existing market or find new markets.

➤ **The marketing mix:** This explains the tactics set out for the 4 Ps.

➤ **The marketing budget:** This outlines how much it will cost to put the marketing strategy and marketing mix tactics into effect.

Here are the advantages and possible drawbacks of a marketing plan:

Advantages	Possible disadvantages
It forces the business to think about what it will try to achieve in the future and which it can judge success against.	Writing it is expensive in terms of managers' time.
The business can be proactive in its marketing rather than reacting to competitors' marketing strategies (more likely with larger businesses).	If not effective, the marketing manager whose plan it is might be reluctant to change it.
It encourages coordination between departments as this will have been considered when drawing up the plan.	Changing external factors may make the plan out of date.

Marketing strategy

A number of factors might affect the market strategy:

➤ Overall business objectives

➤ The nature of the market and how competitive it is

➤ The size and strength of the business

➤ Environmental issues

➤ Technological advances, such as viral marketing campaigns using social media sites.

Marketing budget

This is determined by:

➤ the size of the business

➤ how much money is available

➤ how much is needed to put the strategy into effect

➤ how much revenue from sales is expected

➤ how much competitors are spending

➤ the success or otherwise of past marketing budgets.

Case study

The Superdry brand specialises in street-style clothing aimed at 18–23 year olds. The label was launched in 2003 and has seen rapid growth in the UK and throughout the world. Its marketing strategy has been to develop an image of high quality at affordable prices. The products have  been seen being worn by celebrities and have been made popular by social media sites. The products are easily available in store and online.

The strategy has clearly been very effective with the coordination of the 4 Ps leading to Superdry products being sold in over 100 countries across the world.

Summary

A marketing plan is a detailed report which sets out the marketing objectives for a product. It includes the marketing strategies for the 4 Ps and how they will achieve these marketing objectives.

Market research

Market research is the process of collecting information about the market for a product. The information gathered could be about the whole market, competitors, particular consumers in that market, or it could be about existing or potential customers. There are two types of market research: primary (field) research and secondary (desk) research.

Why carry out market research?

A business needs to keep up to date with the market it is operating in or it will lose sales. This involves gathering data about customer preferences regarding design, price, where to purchase the product and which methods of promotion will appeal.

Market research can help predict likely future changes in demand so that the business can be ready to take advantage of these changes.

Market research is necessary when the business wants to develop new products. There are two types of market research:

Primary research
This is finding new information. It is also known as field research.
Methods include:
• questionnaires: face-to-face, postal, online or by telephone
• interviews, usually face-to-face or by telephone
• focus groups: panels of people who represent a particular market segment. A specialist will lead an open discussion to gather the people's opinions and feelings about a product
• consumer panels: groups of consumers who are asked set questions and then invited to discuss their answers
• observations of consumer behaviour: for example in a shop observing what customers do when deciding what to buy or counting the number of people who pass by a shop (footfall)
• test marketing: trials of a new product can be undertaken and the results analysed before the product launch.

Advantages:	Disadvantages:
• Information focused on consumers (qualitative) • Large amounts of data can be gathered (quantitative) • Information focused on the firm and its specific products/services	• Can be expensive • Takes time to gather and analyse the information • Risk of poorly-phrased questions giving inaccurate answers • Interviewer bias can lead to inaccurate information

Quantitative data is concerned with figures or data which can be measured.

Qualitative data is the opinions of consumers.

Secondary research

This is information which already exists. It is also known as desk research.

Methods include:

• internal sources from records such as company sales records, production information or customer complaints. Information on customer buying habits can be collected from loyalty card data

• external sources such as government population or income statistics, market research reports, commercial publications, trade association information, internet research, company reports.

Advantages:	Disadvantages:
• Cheap to carry out • Data on the whole market can be gathered • Quick to gather data • Several sources can be used to cross-check the data	• Information may be out of date • Information may not be specific to the product • Exact research methods used are not known • Data may be biased, e.g. company reports may have particular data highlighted to company's advantage

Reliability of market research

The accuracy and reliability of the data gathered depends on several factors:

➤ Is the data from a reliable source?

➤ Is the information out of date?

➤ How was the research carried out? Consider sample size and sampling method.

Sampling methods used by researchers

Random sampling: used when a broad range of data on consumers is needed. It allows each member of the target population to have an equal chance of being asked.

Stratified random sampling: only one part (strata) of a population is sampled, perhaps divided by age, gender, interests or by being owners of particular products.

Quota sampling: sets a limit on the strata to be sampled in proportion to the target population, for example 100 men and 100 women to be asked.

Cluster/geographical sampling: when people from a particular geographical area are selected.

Convenience sampling: where people who are easy to ask are used to complete the research.

Analysing the information

The data from the research will be in the form of numerical (quantitative) as well as descriptive (qualitative) data. For it to be analysed, the 'raw' data needs to be converted into a form which can be easily understood and used.

Numerical data is often turned into tables, bar charts, histograms, line graphs or pie charts.

A set of figures can also be analysed using statistical analysis. This could involve finding the **mean** (average number) of a set of data. The **mode** is the number that appears most frequently and the **median** is the middle number of the set of results.

With a normal distribution, the median, mode and mean will all be in the middle at the same point and 50% of the results will lie either side. Standard deviation (SD) measures the spread of marks either side of the mean. This shows how tightly bunched or widely dispersed the results are compared to the mean.

Case study

Kellogg's is the world's leading breakfast cereal producer. Its strategy for growing the business is to broaden its product portfolio. Market research plays a vital part in this. One of Kellogg's most important brands is Crunchy Nut Cornflakes, and Crunchy Nut Bites were introduced to broaden their product portfolio after extensive market research.

Summary

Market research is the collection of data on the consumer, competitors or the market as a whole for a product or service. It includes the collection of original data (primary research) or existing data (secondary research). Once gathered, the data needs to be converted into information that is easy to analyse by using methods such as graphs, charts or statistical analysis.

Markets and customers

A market is where customers and suppliers come together for trade to take place. It is not necessarily a single place but it is where buyers and sellers interact, for example over the internet. Customers are the people who buy a business's products. For a business to be successful, it needs to focus on the needs and wants of consumers in a given market. The size of a market can be measured by the total value of sales from all the businesses that supply that particular good or service.

How is a market defined?

Markets can be divided into four main groups:

➤ Consumer goods, for example cars, breakfast cereals

➤ Producer or industrial goods, for example robots for car production

➤ Consumer services, for example television programmes

➤ Producer or /industrial services, for example delivery services.

There is no easy way to determine a particular market because markets overlap. Adidas, for example, might see itself as being in the sports clothing market but its clothes and shoes will be purchased by a wide range of customers for leisure or fashion. Businesses try to identify the **core market** they are in and promote their products accordingly.

Market size

The size of a market is the total sales of all firms in the market measured in monetary value or the number of units sold. A business will assess whether the total market size is either increasing or decreasing, and why. It will then be ready to react to variations (see: *Economic change*).

Market share

$$\text{Market share} = \frac{\text{sales of the firm in a time period}}{\text{total market sales in the time period}} \times 100$$

$$\text{For example: } \frac{\text{sales of the firm: £100m}}{\text{Total sales for the market: £1,000m}} \times 100 = 10\%$$

Market share allows a firm to measure its success against that of its competitors. The firm can see if it is the market leader or what percentage of the market it has. It may be an objective of the business to increase market share. It is possible for the sales of the firm to increase while its market share falls.

Improving competitiveness

For a business to be successful, it must be competitive. This can be achieved by doing the following:

➤ Lower prices by keeping costs low.

➤ Improve product quality and reinforce this by branding or promotion.

➤ Develop a USP (unique selling point) and reinforce this by branding or promotion.

➤ Develop product innovation from research and development.

➤ Introduce new production techniques so that the products are superior to competitors' products.

➤ Use efficient distribution techniques such as the internet to sell products.

➤ Use effective promotion as part of the marketing strategy.

These are all aimed at gaining and then keeping an advantage over competitors. How easy this is to achieve will often depend on the type of market the firm is operating in:

➤ A market has many firms which are very competitive and it is relatively easy for new firms to enter the market and compete.

➤ A few very large businesses dominate the market and make it difficult for new firms to compete with them.

➤ A market with a single seller is called a monopoly. In this market it is very difficult for other firms to set up in the industry and compete.

The importance of customers

Without customers a business would not survive. The marketing mix (4 Ps) may be aimed at attracting new customers to the business. However, keeping these customers is equally, if not more, important.

To retain customer loyalty, businesses may use marketing activities to establish good relationships. This is called **customer relationship marketing**. Studies have shown that it is between four and ten times more expensive to attract new customers than retain existing ones, so many businesses now focus on customer loyalty.

Instead of the 4 Ps (Price, Place, Product, Promotion), more recently some businesses consider the 4 Cs instead. This puts the consumer at the centre of marketing:

➤ **Cost** – the total cost of owning the product is considered.

➤ **Convenience** – emphasises the ease with which the customer can find and then buy the product.

➤ **Consumer** – the business focuses on satisfying consumer needs.

➤ **Communication** – includes traditional forms of promotion such as advertising, promotional methods and public relations, and also viral advertising or any form of communication between the business and the customer.

Businesses obtain information about their customers and then adapt the marketing mix to suit individual customer needs. Clothing catalogues sent out to customers, for example, contain only the types of clothes the business thinks the customer will be interested in.

The importance of customer service

Having good customer service may distinguish a business from its competitors. A business must be able to judge how successful it is at delivering this.

To measure customer service:

1. Identify the requirements of good customer service.

2. Check this is the same as the customer's idea of good service.

3. Decide how the service will be measured.

4. Implement ways this can be checked on a regular basis.

Poor customer service is likely to lead to loss of customers and bad publicity. Both of these will lead to loss of sales, lower profits and loss of market share to competitors.

Case study

Most car manufacturers use a range of traditional and digital strategies to attract new customers to their brands. A growing number, like Jaguar Land Rover (JLR), are using cutting edge technologies to retain customers too. A spokesperson from JLR's communications department said: "In today's business environment, the best customer is the one you already have. That's why we are making significant efforts to communicate with existing customers."

JLR is doing this by using multiple communication channels: direct mail, email, social media and point-of-sale displays such as brochures.

Summary

A market is where businesses and customers trade. Markets include both consumers and industrial customers for goods and services. The size of a market can be measured and a business can measure its share of that market. To be successful in a market, a business must maintain competitiveness. Customer relationship marketing means putting the customer at the heart of the business to maintain customer loyalty.

Niche & mass markets

Mass markets are large markets for standardised, mass-produced products.

Niche markets are a small market segment of a larger market. The products sold in niche markets are differentiated and are usually sold in small quantities.

Market segments are where sub-groups of a larger market are identified as they share similar characteristics.

The different types of market

A **mass market** is the total market for a product where products are not differentiated by target group, for example toothpaste which is mass produced. The product is:

➤ aimed at a large section of the population

➤ standardised to allow for mass production

➤ often purchased regularly by many consumers, for example baked beans.

A business may identify some parts of the market where particular needs may not be fully met by the standardised product. It may then decide to produce a specific product to target those needs. This will entice specific customers to become brand loyal to these niche products. For example, it may be a toothpaste just for people with sensitive teeth. This is a niche market.

A **niche market** is where the product is:

➤ aimed at one small segment of the market made up of consumers with particular needs or characteristics

➤ differentiated from the product sold to other segments of the market.

An example is wet suits which are produced specifically to meet the needs of scuba divers by specialist businesses.

Here are the benefits and drawbacks of the two types of market:

	Mass market	Niche market
Benefits	• Products produced on a large scale; economies of scale reduce unit costs • More competitive on price • Large market and high sales • Marketing costs relatively more cost effective as spread over high sales	• Small firms can survive in much larger markets • May be a new market not currently being served • Opportunity to sell at a higher price and higher profit margin • Allows a large business to diversify and satisfy customer needs, giving greater satisfaction with the company
Drawbacks	• May not serve the needs of many consumers in the market • Dissatisfaction with a standardised product • Sell at a lower price as standardised product – possibly lower profit margin • Highly competitive market	• No economies of scale, so higher unit costs • May be less competitive as unit costs relatively high • Small market, so increased risk if consumer tastes or fashion change – higher risk for small business

Market segments

To find a niche market a business may first need to use market research to identify the segments of a larger market. Market segments are sub-groups of a larger market and are identified by customers who share similar characteristics.

The market research allows a 'consumer profile' to be drawn up for particular segments; these are often based on age, gender, income, region and interests. This allows the marketing mix to be focused on these consumers.

A market can be segmented in a variety of ways.

Demographic segmentation

This categorises people according to different characteristics, such as gender, age, situation and socio-economic group. Their situation may be: single adult, dual income with or without children, retired with grandchildren, etc. Socio-economic groups A–E are:

E – static income, e.g. unemployed, retired

D – semi-skilled and manual workers

C – skilled manual workers, e.g. cooks

C1 – lower middle, e.g. junior managers, clerical staff

B – middle, e.g. middle managers, professions such as teaching

A – upper/upper middle, e.g. professions such as medicine, law.

Psychographic segmentation

This divides the market by income, occupation and lifestyle. It identifies differences in personalities, values and attitudes as well as in lifestyle. For example, this might be by:

➤ **religion:** Atheist, Buddhist, Christian, Hindu, Jew, Muslim, Sikh

➤ **interests:** cooking, gardening, health, holidays, home improvements, sports, water sports.

Geographic segmentation

This divides the market into different regions with different characteristics. Global companies might split the global market by different countries with different cultures/buying habits.

Why it is useful to segment a market

Segmentation allows a business to develop a marketing mix to target these consumers more specifically. This will allow more cost-efficient marketing. In addition, the product is more likely to meet the specific needs of consumers and therefore be more successful.

Case study

Pink Ladies is a members-only taxi service aimed at women. All the drivers are female and wear a distinctive uniform. The aim of the business is to provide a service which allays women's fears about getting home after a night out. The taxi drivers text the women to let them know they have arrived outside so the women do not have to stand in the street alone. This is a niche market which meets the specific needs of women.

Summary

Mass markets are large markets for standardised, mass-produced products. Niche markets have differentiated products usually sold in small market segments. Identifying the types of customers in these markets allows a business to target its marketing mix more effectively.

Place and e-commerce

Place is part of the marketing mix. It involves decisions by a business on how and where the product should be sold to the customer. These decisions should result in using the best channel of distribution to get the right product to the right customer at the right price. The channel of distribution is comprised of the intermediaries through which a product will pass from the producer to the consumer.

Channels of distribution

The best channel of distribution is usually one which reaches as wide a market as possible and via as few intermediaries as possible, since each intermediary will want to make a profit. Channels include:

Direct from the producer to the consumer: suitable for products which require direct links to the consumer, for detailed explanation, advice, or other services. Examples include: specialist computer software, hairdressing services, fitted kitchens.

Producer → retailer → consumer: suitable for standardised products that are supplied to many customers. Rather than supplying large quantities direct to consumers, it is more cost efficient to sell to retailers who combine these with the products from other producers. An example is clothing.

Producer → wholesaler → retailer → consumer: suitable for some products produced in large quantities and sold to a wide range of consumers. The wholesaler breaks the bulk quantities of the products down into smaller quantities which are suitable for small retailers to purchase, thereby reducing the administration and distribution costs of the producer.

Producer → agent → wholesaler → retailer → consumer: suitable if a producer wants to supply its products to a foreign market. The agent provides specific knowledge and advice about the market so that the product is more likely to be successful.

Other factors affecting choice include: selling only to other businesses; perishability; the nature of the market and after-sales service required.

Recent trends

➤ Increased e-tailing rather than retailing has meant big changes for delivery companies as the goods are purchased online and then delivered to the customer by other businesses.

➤ Increasing use of the internet has meant that more and more services are sold directly from the producer to the consumer rather than via intermediaries.

E-commerce

E-commerce is the buying and selling of goods or services electronically or over the internet. It has become increasingly important due to the growth in ownership of electronic devices and mobile phones, and the facility to pay online using electronic funds transfer. This is called business to consumer (B2C) trade.

E-commerce also includes business to business (B2B) trade. It is quicker, cheaper and easier to both find and buy from suppliers worldwide.

Benefits	Drawbacks
• Access to a global market	• Security issues over identity fraud and secure payment methods
• Business location can be footloose as no need to be near to its market	
	• Hackers may steal business ideas
• 24/7 trading possible	• Business website may not be easy to locate as so many others on the internet
• Reduced need for retail outlets cuts costs	
• Automated purchasing and direct payment reduces the need for staff, so cuts wage costs	• Increased competition from other businesses at home and abroad
	• Easier for consumers to compare prices between businesses. Constant monitoring required by the business increases costs
• Easier for consumers to compare prices across different websites	
• The long tail distribution* makes it cost effective to sell small quantities of a large number of products. This brings high sales from many items rather than sales from a few popular items	• Shipping costs and delays in delivery may cause discontent amongst customers

* Where the bulk of sales in a market is made up from the sales of a few products, the 'long tail' is the many smaller, niche products that make up the rest of the market.

Case study

Alibaba.com is an online shopping website for small businesses to sell their products directly to other businesses and consumers. It started in China in 1998 and has spread to many Asian countries. Originally it was for business to business (B2B) trade, but it has since expanded to include business to consumer (B2C) and consumer to consumer (C2C) trade. The growth in e-commerce has reduced the intermediaries in the channels of distribution for many businesses and the success of this site is testament to the continued popularity of online trade.

Summary

Place is the part of the marketing mix which assesses how to get the product to the consumer. It involves choosing the most suitable channel of distribution to use in order to reach the target market and make sales.

Price

Price is the amount a business charges a customer for a product. It helps to determine the sales and profits made by the business. There are a number of pricing strategies and the strategy selected needs to fit in with the rest of the marketing mix. It might be assumed that customers always want to pay the lowest prices but this is not always true. The price can add to the product's image.

Factors affecting price

➤ **Demand and supply:** if prices are high, the quantity demanded is usually lower. Lower prices often increase market share.

➤ **Marketing objectives:** to increase market share, a business may use a pricing strategy which gives increased sales.

➤ **Marketing mix:** the price must fit in with the rest of the mix.

➤ **Stage of the product life cycle:** the pricing strategy will depend on which stage the product is in.

➤ **Cost of production:** all costs of production must be covered if the business is to make a profit.

➤ **Target market:** whether target customers are in high or low income groups.

➤ **Nature of the market:** whether the market is very competitive or not.

➤ **Exchange rates:** products sold in overseas markets are affected by exchange rate changes. Businesses could follow the changes or leave prices in export markets unchanged. (See: *Economic change* and *Business strategy.*)

➤ **Laws and regulations:** taxes and government policies can affect prices.

Cost-based pricing strategies

Cost-plus pricing: cost per unit is calculated and then a certain percentage profit is added to give the price. This is also called **full-cost** or **absorption pricing**.

Contribution-cost (or **marginal cost**) **pricing:** only variable costs are taken into account and any extra revenue makes a contribution to the fixed costs.

Advantages	**Cost-plus:** Easy to calculate for single product, and suitable for uncompetitive markets
	Contribution-cost: Suitable for competitive markets
Disadvantages	**Cost-plus:** Difficult to calculate for multi-product firms, and unsuitable for competitive markets
	Contribution-cost: Profit only recorded when total contribution exceeds fixed costs

Examples:

Cost-plus pricing: A firm produces 1,000 units per week. Fixed costs are £5,000 per week and the variable cost per unit is £10. If the firm want a mark-up of 50% the price would be:

£5,000/1,000 = £5 per unit plus £10 variable cost = £15. Adding the 50% mark-up gives a selling price of £22.50.

Contribution-cost pricing: Variable cost = £10. Fixed costs per year are £260,000. If the selling price is £20, each product sold makes a contribution to fixed costs of £10. The firm would have to sell 26,000 products for all fixed costs to be covered. Further sales would bring a profit.

Competitor-based pricing

Competitive pricing: price is set around the same level as other products in the market.

Price leadership: price is set higher than competitors to reinforce a brand image.

Loss leaders: price is set below cost to attract customers then entice them to buy other products. Used by supermarkets.

Destroyer pricing: price is set low to drive out competitors.

Price discrimination: price is set at different levels for the same product. To be effective the market must be separated in some way, e.g. age or time. Uses knowledge of elasticity of demand (or price sensitivity of customers) to charge different prices so that total revenue can be increased.

Dynamic pricing: price is constantly adjusted depending on the level of demand. This is a strategy increasingly used by online businesses so they can track customer buying habits and charge prices according to what customers are prepared to pay.

Advantages	• Competes with existing products
	• Increases sales or sales remain high
	• Reduces competition
	• Increases market share
	• Sales revenue may be maximised for price discrimination and dynamic pricing
	• Profits are higher using dynamic pricing
Disadvantages	• Profits are sacrificed if prices are kept lower but they are higher using dynamic pricing
	• Sales revenue may not be maximised for all of these strategies apart from price discrimination and dynamic pricing
	• Costs of researching competitors' prices
	• Administrative costs of having different prices for dynamic pricing
	• Customers may resent paying higher prices using dynamic pricing and look for alternatives

New product pricing strategy

Skimming or creaming: price is set high for a new unique product.

Penetration pricing: price is set lower than the existing products in the market in order to enter a competitive market.

Advantages	**Skimming:**
	• Endorses brand image of high quality and originality
	• Suitable for a highly-differentiated product
	• Maximises short-term profits before competitors enter the market
	Penetration pricing:
	• Maximises sales revenue when product launched
	• Encourages customers to try new product
	• Used when mass marketing and aiming for a large market share
Disadvantages	**Skimming:**
	• High price deters potential sales
	• Attracts competitors to launch similar product
	Penetration pricing:
	• Low profit margins are likely

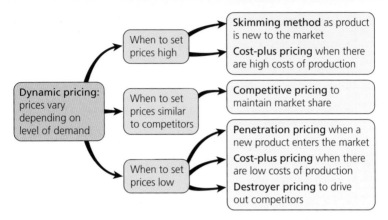

In a competitive market prices are set by demand and supply. If demand is very responsive to price changes, this would be called **price elastic demand**. Any percentage change in price would lead to a larger percentage change in quantity demanded.

However, if the demand is **price inelastic**, that means that consumers are not price sensitive.

	Elastic demand	Inelastic demand
Increase in price	revenue down	revenue up
Decrease in price	revenue up	revenue down

Demand tends to be price elastic if:

➤ there are many close substitutes

➤ price is a small proportion of consumer income

➤ the product is not a necessity.

However, elasticity is hard to measure and a business may not be sure of the exact elasticity of demand for its product. The other complication is that it will change quite regularly as other factors in the economy change.

Case study

Derby County Football Club has a dynamic pricing strategy and prices its tickets according to the popularity of the game. The price of tickets is determined by computer servers in Indiana and prices move up or down depending on demand. This strategy was used by airlines to determine the price of flights, but is now being used  by theatres and sporting venues all over the world. The drawback is that people are unhappy when they find out they have paid a much higher price than the person sitting next to them!

Summary

The price of a product is an important part of the marketing mix. It can affect the image of the product and how well it sells. There are several pricing strategies which a business can use depending on the rest of the marketing mix and the marketing objectives. However, in a competitive market the price is determined by where supply equals demand.

Product life cycle

A product is a good or service which satisfies a consumer need and for which the consumer is prepared to pay a price. It is the starting point of the marketing mix, for without a good or service the rest of the marketing mix is pointless.

A product life cycle is the pattern of sales a product will usually follow from its research and development through to its being withdrawn from the market.

What is a product?

A product may be:

➤ a tangible **good**, something you can touch

➤ a **service**, which is an intangible good, something you cannot touch, such as mobile phone messaging

➤ sold directly to consumers and therefore a **consumer good**, such as Cadbury's chocolate bars

➤ sold to producers, i.e. other businesses. This is called a **producer good**. An example is a business providing lorry freight services.

For a product to be successful, it needs to:

➤ fulfil consumer needs as identified from market research, e.g. a pair of trainers should be comfortable to wear

➤ appeal to consumers as well as performing its function well, e.g. well-designed kitchen equipment

➤ conform to any legal requirements and be environmentally friendly, e.g. babies' toys should not have small parts which could be swallowed and should have packaging which is recyclable

➤ have a price affordable to the target market, e.g. the price of cinema admissions should be within the budget of young people

➤ have a unique selling point (USP) which makes it stand out from competing products. Having a USP helps create a brand image, hopefully leading to brand loyalty.

A brand is anything which differentiates the product from the competition. It is created by using a unique name, image, trademark, tune, symbol, colour or design. A successful brand will develop brand loyal customers. The most successful brands are recognised and purchased all over the world.

Product life cycle

All products go through different stages of sales over time. The stages are always the same but the speed depends on the market and type of product, so the shape will vary. A business needs to consider each product's stage of the life cycle so that their portfolio of products will contain products at each stage.

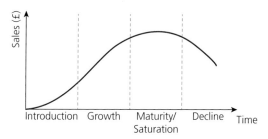

Introduction: Sales may grow slowly and there are no competitors. Decisions are taken on pricing. Promotion is informative to make consumers aware of the product's existence. Place may be restricted to a limited number of outlets. Cash flow is probably negative, with more costs being spent than income coming in from sales.

Growth: If the product is successful, sales grow rapidly. Promotion focuses on creating a brand image to encourage repeat purchases. The product is sold through more outlets. The pricing strategy may change to competitive as similar products come onto the market. The product may be improved to maintain appeal and keep repeat sales. The development costs and heavy advertising costs may mean that cash flow is still negative.

Maturity and saturation: Sales stabilise. Maturity is where sales growth is slow; saturation is where there are few, if any, new consumers, so sales are repeat sales. Saturation may last for many years, such as Cadbury's Dairy Milk. For technology or fashion products, where change can occur rapidly, it may last less than a year. Promotion is still focused on reinforcing the brand image. Pricing is still likely to be competitive as there may be many other products in the market. Cash flow is positive as sales are at their highest.

Extension strategies: These are to extend the maturity stage of the life cycle. They include increasing demand by developing new markets abroad for the existing product, finding new uses for the existing product, changing the product slightly to appeal to different markets, and developing a wider range of products. The life cycle graph might look like this:

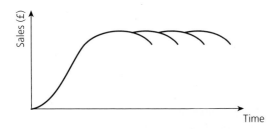

Decline: Sales decline steadily if extension strategies are not used or are not successful. The price may be lowered to sell off remaining stock. Promotion is likely to be limited, with simple advertising about reduced prices. The number of outlets reduces as sales fall and the product stops being produced. The cash flow may still be positive for some time as advertising costs fall but sales fall slowly.

Using product life cycles

A business can use product life cycles to:

➤ identify when a product should be withdrawn or a new product introduced

➤ help plan its product portfolio (mix of products)

➤ show when it needs to consider using extension strategies

➤ decide when to increase spending on advertising or research and development of new products

➤ decide when pricing strategies need to be changed

➤ decide when to change the promotion.

Developing new products

New products are usually developed via the following process:

Generation of new ideas and idea screening: Research and development identifies ideas for new products which are then narrowed down.

Concept development, analysis and testing: This narrows down the ideas further by looking at a possible target market, the features which should be incorporated, what it will cost to produce and the possible impact of the new products on the company's overall costs, sales revenue and profits (see: *Boston Matrix*).

Product development: A prototype is developed. Focus groups may research possible consumer reaction.

Test marketing: The new product is launched in a small section of the market. Consumer feedback is sought and sales analysed. The need for changes will be assessed and incorporated into the product before final launch in the main market.

Commercialisation and launch: The final version of the new product is launched.

Businesses will need to take steps to protect new products from being copied. This may involve taking out a patent to stop competitors copying the design.

Case study

In 2009, Rowntree's (owned by Nestlé) launched the sweets Randoms. These are natural fruit-flavoured jelly sweets in unique shapes such as musical notes, ice-cream cones and flowers. The launch seemed to have been successful with sales quickly growing.

In 2013, Squidgy Speak, an extension to Randoms, was launched. These are fruit-flavoured foamy sweets aimed at 16–24 year olds.

Summary

A product is a good or a service which satisfies consumer needs. It is one of the 4 Ps of the marketing mix. All products go through different stages of the product life cycle. Product life cycles help a business to identify when to develop or withdraw products.

Promotion

This is the part of the marketing mix which informs consumers about a product or service and then persuades them to buy it. The two main types of promotion are advertising and sales promotion. Both of these can be broken down further to enable a comprehensive mixture of promotional techniques to be used to sell a product, i.e. the promotional mix.

Sales promotions

These are usually short term and aimed at encouraging customers to change their buying habits. Customers who feel they have a bargain will try the new products and hopefully become brand loyal.

Types of sales promotion include:

Advertising

Advertising can be:

➤ informative, where the focus of the message is to provide details about the product for the consumer

➤ persuasive, where the intention is to encourage the consumer to purchase the product and foster brand loyalty with repeat purchases.

Here is a summary of ways and places to advertise a product:

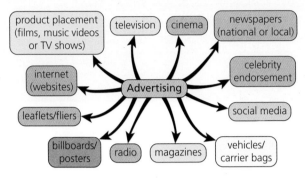

AIDA and DAGMAR

AIDA stands for:

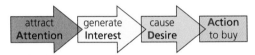

This summarises the stages a customer goes through if the advertising is successful.

DAGMAR stands for Defining Advertising Goals for Measured Advertising Results. This means the business will set clear and measurable goals to test whether the advertising is effective, for example sales increased by 3% or product awareness increased (tested by market research).

Other methods of promotion

Other methods of promotion include the following:

➤ Public relations and sponsorship are both similar to advertising as they are aimed at getting a message across to the consumer. For example, Coca-Cola sponsored the 2012 Olympic Games to emphasise energy and youth.

➤ Personal selling is where one-to-one selling takes place at the point of sale with the aim of building a relationship with the customer and encouraging repeat sales.

➤ Direct mail is sent to people's houses to inform and encourage a purchase.

➤ Trade fairs and exhibitions are usually aimed at business customers.

➤ Viral marketing uses social media sites. For example, Burberry has YouTube and Facebook views as well as a large number of followers on Twitter. Tweetwalk was launched with Twitter to be the first to show consumers images of new clothing collections.

The promotional mix chosen will depend on the **marketing objectives** for the product. Is the business trying to:

➤ increase sales

➤ launch a new product on the market

➤ retain existing customers

➤ reinforce a brand image

➤ reinforce a unique selling point (USP)?

Factors affecting the promotional mix

➤ **Type of product:** whether a consumer good, producer good (products sold to other businesses B2B), consumer service or producer service.

➤ **New product or not:** Consumers will not buy a new product if they do not know it exists. The business may use advertising and also sales promotion to encourage consumers to try the new product.

➤ **Target market:** The type of media will depend on the target market at which the product is aimed. If the product is aimed at the mass market, TV and national newspapers may be appropriate but for small specialist markets magazines may be more suitable.

➤ **Nature of the product:** Regularly consumed products will have advertising to reinforce brand image and promotions to ensure repeat sales.

➤ **Size of the marketing budget:** A small business will not have a budget large enough for TV or national newspapers.

➤ **Types of competitor promotion:** If competitors are using loyalty cards, a business may have to do the same.

➤ **Nature of the brand image being created:** If the business wants to create an exclusive brand image it will not use promotional methods such as BOGOF.

➤ **Global marketing:** The whole marketing strategy will need to be different if the product is marketed globally. The types of advertising used, sponsorship, product placement in globally-screened films and celebrity endorsement may all be considered.

Case study

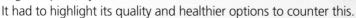

An estimated £1bn was spent by official sponsors of the 2012 Olympic Games. Coca-Cola and McDonald's were two of the 11 global firms paying an estimated £61m. Adidas were providers of the official sportswear.

Social media was used to track messages on sites such as Twitter, YouTube and Facebook; Adidas came out top as the most talked about brand. However, McDonald's saw negative publicity as it was not seen as the food of athletes. It had to highlight its quality and healthier options to counter this.

Summary

Promotion is concerned with raising awareness for a product in the mind of target consumers, then encouraging them to purchase. It can take the form of advertising or sales promotion methods which encourage consumers to try a new product or remain brand loyal. Advertising can be either informative or persuasive. AIDA and DAGMAR are techniques to check the effectiveness of promotional methods.

Sales forecasting

Sales forecasting is estimating the future level of sales of goods and services. Companies must plan production, cash flow, stock levels and labour needs to ensure they keep costs low. To do this they need to predict future sales as accurately as possible. If the forecast is too low, they will have lost the opportunity to increase sales. If it is too high, they will have produced more than they can sell.

Quantitative methods of sales forecasting

Future sales can be predicted as a straightforward extrapolation of past sales. However, this may not be accurate as the sales pattern may change – past performance is not always a reliable indicator of future sales.

Time-series analysis: This method uses past sales figures to predict future sales. The actual sales figures can vary due to:

➤ **the trend:** the underlying movement in the figures in a time-series

➤ **seasonal fluctuations:** regular and repeated variations in the sales figures over a 12-month period

➤ **cyclical fluctuations:** variations in the sales figures which occur over a longer period of time, i.e. more than a year, due to the trade cycle

➤ **random fluctuations:** unpredictable variations in the sales figures caused by unusual events such as a spell of snow causing sales of wellington boots to increase.

Apart from random fluctuations, these variations can have their fluctuations 'smoothed out' by a method called **moving averages**. This will find the short-term trend in the figures which is likely to be more accurate as factors such as seasonal factors will have been averaged out. Look at this example for sales of jewellery for a small retailer.

Year/Quarter	Sales revenue	Quarterly centred moving average (trend)	Seasonal variation (difference between the actual sales revenue and the trend)
Year 1 1st quarter	100		
Year 1 2nd quarter	120		
Year 1 3rd quarter	150	116.25	33.75
Year 1 4th quarter	90	118.75	−28.75
Year 2 1st quarter	110	117.5	−7.5
Year 2 2nd quarter	130	116.25	13.75
Year 2 3rd quarter	130		
Year 2 4th quarter	100		

All figures in thousands

Correlation

Another statistical method which can be applied to data is to calculate whether there is a relationship between two sets of figures. Consider these two graphs.

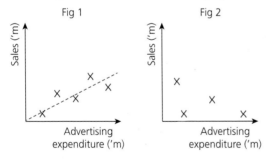

Fig. 1 has a positive correlation, i.e. it shows that when advertising expenditure increases so do sales, and a line of best fit has been added to show this. Fig. 2 appears to have no such relationship. However, a correlation does not **prove** that a relationship exists and further research might be needed.

Correlations are useful when trying to establish links between figures such as sales, prices and competitors' promotional spending. Marketing managers can then use this information to inform their own decisions about the marketing strategy to adopt.

Qualitative methods of sales forecasting

These involve expert opinion and customer feedback and are used where there is insufficient numerical data available or where data becomes out of date due to a rapidly-changing market.

Sales-force composite: Sales staff are asked for their forecast of sales based on their contact with customers. These are added together to form a total forecast for the product. This is quick and cheap to implement but may not take into account external influences on sales; also, sales staff might be over-optimistic. This method is suitable if selling directly to customers, but less helpful for online sales.

Consumer surveys: Market research methods are used to predict customer buying habits. It can be carried out by the business itself but is time consuming and a specialist market research agency may be used instead.

Delphi method: A detailed questionnaire is sent out to a selected group of independent experts who comment on factors they think might affect future sales. The results are collated and sent back for the experts to reconsider their forecasts. This will bring the views of the experts closer together and be more accurate.

Jury of experts: This is similar to the Delphi method but involves a group of experts from within the business who meet to develop forecasts based on their specific knowledge of the business. It is quicker and cheaper than the Delphi method but lacks views on external factors.

Problems with accuracy

➤ Market research results not carried out by experts.

➤ Sales teams may overestimate future sales.

➤ Past trends are no guarantee of future sales.

➤ External factors may affect sales.

➤ Consumer trends change or fashion changes.

➤ New technology, new inventions and products.

Case study

Clothing for larger ladies is boosting the fashion industry with sales of plus-size clothing increasing to $5 billion. Sizes 16 to 32 need to be produced and sold to cater for the larger size of British women. Web-based retailers, such as Very and ASOS, are launching a supersize, flattering range of clothes based on forecasts about future sales of larger sizes. Without sales forecasting, these businesses may miss out on opportunities to increase sales.

Summary

Sales forecasting helps to reduce costs and ensure potential sales are not missed. Quantitative statistical methods predict trends in sales. Qualitative methods predict sales using the opinions of consumers and experts from inside or outside the business.

SWOT analysis

SWOT stands for Strengths, Weaknesses, Opportunities and Threats. It is a way of analysing both the internal and the external factors that may affect any major strategic decision being taken by a business, such as new product development.

Strengths and weaknesses

Internal factors affecting any major strategic decision are the strengths and weaknesses of the business itself. The business does have some control over these internal factors as they are within its capability to change.

Strengths can include:

➤ adequate retained profit or an ability to attract finance

➤ existing expertise of employees

➤ existing logistics and outlet networks and good links with suppliers

➤ the capacity of existing equipment to produce the new product.

Weaknesses can include:

➤ a high gearing ratio making it difficult to attract additional finance

➤ production facilities at maximum capacity

➤ high labour turnover leading to lack of skilled staff.

Opportunities and threats

External factors affecting strategic decisions are the opportunities and threats from outside influences which are not within the control of the business.

Opportunities may include:

➤ a gap in the market

➤ being in the boom phase of the business cycle

➤ new technological developments

➤ new research, for example into health factors, creating new demand

➤ government policy changing

➤ the development of new emerging markets creating opportunities to market products abroad and decrease production costs.

Threats may include:

➤ recession

➤ increased taxation on particular products

➤ decreased supply of resources

➤ increased costs of raw materials and transport

➤ increased competition

➤ changes in fashion/trends.

Uses of SWOT analysis

A business might use SWOT analysis to:

➤ aid the planning and decision-making process when launching a new product. It enables the business to consider the impact of a wide range of factors when deciding on the marketing mix.

➤ analyse the development of extension strategies for an existing product which has entered the mature phase of its product life cycle

➤ launch an existing product into a new market or diversify the product range.

➤ assess whether to take over another business with a similar product range (horizontal integration).

SWOT analysis is an essential element in strategic analysis. Unless a business knows where it is at present (in terms of both its internal and its external environment) it will not be able to make effective strategic choices to allow the business to move towards future objectives.

Benefits of SWOT analysis

➤ It enables a business to assess all the internal and external factors which will affect the success of a particular strategic decision.

➤ It enables the business to identify possible problems with a new product and so develop strategies to avoid possible difficulties.

➤ Thorough analysis of these internal and external factors means that the chosen marketing mix is likely to be more successful. Any difficulties will have largely been identified and possibly avoided.

➤ The best sources of finance will have been identified, making the strategic decision more cost effective and likely to succeed.

Drawbacks of SWOT analysis

➤ A detailed analysis takes time and can be expensive to carry out.

➤ It is time specific and may quickly become outdated.

➤ It is only useful if sufficient time and money have been devoted to the analysis.

Case study

SWOT to build a new velodrome at Pride Park, Derby
The project is being developed by Derby City Council.

Strengths: existing good reputation for working with the local community; good brand image locally; land owned by Derby County Football Club currently not being used; building on existing partnerships between Derby County Football Club and Derby City Council to provide additional car parking space for football supporters.

Weaknesses: lack of staff expertise in cycling; difficulties in raising finance as cuts in budgets at Derby City Council.

Opportunities: increased popularity of cycling after the successes of the Olympics and Tour de France in 2012; increased government funding to the sport of cycling; good infrastructure already existing on Pride Park; only one other velodrome in the country, which is far away from this area.

Threats: recession and high government debt may lead to cuts in funding; increased building costs leading to insufficient funding to complete the project.

Summary

SWOT analysis is a useful tool to help a business establish its internal strengths and weaknesses, and external opportunities and threats, before considering important strategic choices that will affect its future success. It makes the business consider a wide range of factors before choosing between possible strategic options. It also improves planning to avoid any potential difficulties identified during the process.

Lean production

Lean production is concerned with producing high quality goods and services but with the minimum of waste. By keeping waste to a minimum, costs are kept down and the firm becomes more competitive. Lean production as a production technique was first developed by Japanese manufacturers and mostly applies to manufacturing not service industries.

Sources of waste

There are various sources of waste in industry:

➤ Excessive transportation of components or products around the factory or warehouse

➤ Excessive holding of stock

➤ Too much movement of people between operations on the production line

➤ Waiting time between stages in the production process

➤ Over-production, where products are produced before they are required

➤ Over-processing: using a manufacturing process for goods which is more complicated than is required

➤ Defective goods.

Lean production techniques

Simultaneous engineering
The different stages required to develop a new product, such as market research, design, engineering, and costing the product, are all carried out at the same time. The firm can get a new product to market more quickly than competitors who do not use this process.

Cell production

Flow production is changed so that instead of a continuous production line, production is broken down into a series of self-contained units or cells. Each cell completes a particular stage of the production process. The team leader and workers are responsible for that entire stage of production and for ensuring production targets are met. The workers have a sense of responsibility and feel valued, but they need to be trained and multi-skilled.

Time-based management

This involves reducing both the length of time taken to produce the product and the lead time (the time between the customer placing an order and the finished product being delivered). The production process is flexible to meet differing customer demand. A business will usually need adaptable machinery, multi-skilled workers and sometimes flexible employment contracts.

Just-in-time stock control (JIT)

Components arrive at the production line at the exact point they are needed. For this to be successful, the business must have close links with its suppliers. Storage costs are cut as there is no need to have warehouse space for stocks, liquidity improves, and it is less likely that stocks will be damaged. However, ordering costs increase and any supplier production or delivery problems will halt production.

Kaizen (continuous improvement)

This arises from the belief that everyone can contribute to improving the process. In fact, workers are thought to know more than managers about ways to reduce waste or improve production techniques. For businesses using this technique, management must embrace this philosophy when managing employees, and workers must feel part of the team and valued. The acceptance of Kaizen needs to be at **all** levels of the business to work effectively.

Advantages of lean production	Potential limitations
• Avoids waste in time and resources	• May require expensive machinery such as robots to carry out actions
• Unit costs are reduced	
• Prices can be reduced/profits increased	• Requires commitment of all employees including managers
• New products are launched more quickly.	• Less likely to be available for small businesses (lack of capital)
• Working capital not tied up in stock	
• Higher quality products	• Retraining of staff may be expensive
• Improved motivation	• Difficult to react to sudden increases in demand as stocks are low
• Higher productivity levels	

Case study

Jaguar produce a range of luxury cars which are exported all over the world. The company identified the production processes which added most value so that any which did not could be eliminated.

The company changed to workers operating in small teams with a team leader. The teams were trained in using new approaches and tools. Just-in-time was also introduced so workers press a button and more stocks are delivered just before they need to be fitted to the next car. Stocks are delivered to the factory several times a day.

Jaguar has already eliminated many sources of waste in its factory but the process is continuous. The approach has enabled Jaguar to reduce the time needed to produce each car, and these principles of production have been used as a benchmark elsewhere.

Summary

Lean production is concerned with reducing waste at all levels in a business. Techniques include simultaneous engineering, cell production, time-based management, JIT and Kaizen. Lean production is not suitable for all businesses as it is expensive to introduce.

Location

Locating business activity is when the business is deciding where to set up for the first time or when it is expanding or relocating. It is a strategic decision for the long term so it is taken at the highest management level of the business. Managers will consider both quantitative and qualitative factors in order to select the optimal location.

The importance of location

Location is important when a business is:

➤ setting up for the first time

➤ an established business that wants to relocate

➤ an established business that wants to expand

➤ seeking more modern facilities

➤ wanting to lower costs by reducing some of its input costs, which could lead to relocation abroad.

The costs and benefits of each site need to be assessed before a decision is taken.

Quantitative factors

These are financial measures which have a direct impact on costs or revenues, and hence on profits. They include the following:

➤ Land and other one-off set-up costs – such as rent, building costs or refurbishment. City centre sites will be more expensive then out-of-town sites.

➤ Closeness to the market or sales revenue potential – for retail businesses, the footfall (number of people going into a shop in a given period of time) is vital in determining sales revenue.

➤ Transport costs – if a business needs quick access to raw materials or components, this will be a significant factor. Some businesses use **JIT** (see: *Lean production*) and suppliers must be nearby or easily accessible.

➤ Labour – the availability of labour, with the right skills, will be important to labour-intensive operations.

➤ Government grants – these are given in many countries to attract businesses to a particular area.

➤ Technological factors – such as whether employees can carry out their work from home, or whether the business itself sells online.

Qualitative factors

These are non-measurable factors and include:

➤ Potential for further expansion – potential development opportunities in the future may be a factor.

➤ Social, environmental and ethical considerations – pressure groups may object to a business locating in an area if it may damage the region or produce waste.

➤ Owner preference – small businesses may choose to locate in an area where the owner chooses to live.

➤ Laws and regulations – ease of obtaining any necessary planning permission from local government will also be considered.

Multi-site locations

This is where a business operates from more than one location. Large companies, including multinationals, may have many sites. These are often service sector businesses, but manufacturing businesses may also find it beneficial to operate from several sites as doing so minimises the chance of disruption if there is a problem at one site.

Locating abroad

A business deciding where to locate abroad has additional factors to consider, such as reducing costs, gaining access to new markets or overcoming trade barriers.

Case study

In 2011, the Philippines overtook India as the country with the largest number of call centre staff – over 600,000. They work mainly at night when the rest of the world is awake. Businesses are locating their booking offices and customer service centres in the Philippines as wages are low there, most Filipinos speak English and international calls are no longer expensive. Telephone systems using the internet (IP telephony such as Skype) have brought down costs still further.

Summary

Choosing where to locate is a key decision for a business. Quantitative (financial) factors are important in determining the potential profitability of the site. Qualitative (not quantifiable in terms of money) factors are also important. Large businesses often operate from many sites. There are additional factors when choosing an overseas location.

Producing goods

Producing goods is the process of using inputs and changing them into outputs or products. There are several different methods of production from which a business can choose. A business will decide how many goods to produce or customers to serve and then it will choose which method of production to use: job, batch, flow or mass customisation.

Initial decisions

Decisions about producing goods involve different departments, such as marketing (to discuss what to produce and the likely demand for the product), finance (to see if there is sufficient cash to pay for the production) and Human Resources (to see if employees with the right skills are available for production).

The business must decide: what product to produce (see: *Market research*); what production method to use; where production should take place (see: *Location*); and what resources the business has at its disposal and how it can ensure quality is maintained (see: *Quality*).

The operations manager will decide what methods of production to use when producing the goods.

Production methods

The main methods of production are:

Method	Description	Advantages	Disadvantages
Job production, e.g. house extension, wedding cake, motorway, Aston Martin car	One-off items produced to the specific design of a customer. A single product is made before the next one is started.	• High worker motivation as more variety in tasks • Unique product matches needs to specific customer • High price can be charged • High value added	• High set-up costs • Skilled labour often required as labour-intensive • Takes a long time to complete • High labour costs • Flexible production facilities required

Method	Description	Advantages	Disadvantages
Batch production, e.g. shoes of a particular size and style, bakeries with particular types of bread	Relatively small quantity of identical products produced – every unit goes through one process before passing on to next stage.*	• Less skilled labour required as focus on one or two operations • Uses more standardised machinery • Can supply larger market than job production • Flexibility to change batch to meet customer requirements	• Standardised product • Careful planning and coordination needed for efficient production • Can lead to high stock levels when items wait to move between processes • If batches are small, unit costs are relatively high • Demotivating for workers
Flow (mass) production, e.g. bottles of Coca-Cola, breakfast cereals, baked beans, Cadbury's chocolates	Items produced on large scale. Production moves continually from one stage to the next.	• Large output produced • Cost per unit low (economies of scale) • Prices low • Often unskilled or semi-skilled labour • Highly automated production • JIT stock control used • Quality high as easy to check products passing through production process	• Monotonous for workforce • May have to pay higher wages or suffer high labour turnover and absenteeism • High capital investment • Standardised product produced • Little flexibility with plant and equipment to produce other products • Breakdowns costly as whole production line stops until problem is fixed
Mass customisation, e.g. Ford Focus (colour, interior specification, etc.), NIKEiD sportswear, Dell computers	Produced to individual customer requirements but using computer-aided production systems giving mass production cost levels.	• Low costs but still meets individual customer needs • Uses CAD/CAM techniques • Uses many standard components to keep costs low	• Product redesign might be needed and this can be expensive • Expensive capital to facilitate flexibility – usually computer controlled • Needs flexible and multi-skilled labour

* Not the same as 'batches of flow production', where a large quantity of the product is produced continuously and another product is made on the production line afterwards.

Choice of production method will depend on:

➤ the capital available to the business

➤ the nature of the product

➤ the size of the market

➤ the state of technology.

Case study

NIKEiD is a service provided by Nike, the sportswear company, which allows customers to customise their shoes as they purchase them. The personalised shoes can be ordered online and from some stores. The number of people accessing this online is 15 million and it has seen sales revenue rise rapidly to about 20% of store revenue. This is a success story for mass customisation.

Summary

Producing goods involves using inputs to produce outputs or products. Chosen methods of production can be job, batch, flow or mass customisation. Businesses need to choose carefully which method is most suitable for their products.

Productivity & efficiency

Production is the process of managing manufacturing or service output to meet customer needs. Total production levels can be measured in terms of the number of units (or value of them) produced in a certain time period.

Productivity is a measure of the number of inputs a business uses to produce a given output. Efficiency is producing this output using the smallest possible amount of inputs.

Organising resources

Organising resources to ensure that production is carried out at the lowest possible cost is important to maximise profits. Operations managers are responsible for:

➤ deciding which production methods to use and what level of machinery, labour, etc. is required

➤ what level of capacity utilisation to use

➤ what stock levels to maintain

➤ how best to ensure quality

➤ how to ensure the output is produced efficiently.

Capacity utilisation

A service sector business might use measures such as length of queues or time taken to respond to customer queries to check if they are working at maximum capacity. A manufacturing business measures actual output as a percentage of maximum possible output. Full capacity is 100%. Any less means the firm could increase its output.

Low capacity utilisation due to a permanent fall in demand might lead to the firm reducing excess capacity by moving to cheaper premises or not replacing workers. If the fall is temporary, the firm could try to increase demand through advertising, price promotions, etc. Making changes to capacity is a strategic decision for a business.

Benefits of working at full capacity	Drawbacks of working at full capacity
• Fixed costs are spread over a greater output so the fixed cost per unit falls. Fixed cost per unit is at the lowest level possible at 100% capacity • Variable costs may be low due to discounts from bulk purchasing of raw materials/components • Lower unit costs result in either higher profits or lower prices, therefore improving competitiveness • Image of a successful firm given to stakeholders • Job security for employees increased	• Firm cannot cope with additional demand so orders may be lost • Increased unit costs as fixed cost per unit will not be at a minimum • Higher prices/lower profits • Pressure on machinery – no time for maintenance • Pressure on employees – absences cause problems • Little or no time for employee training • May be less focus on developing new products as focus is on current products

Productivity

To ensure low unit costs, managers must keep control of resources and monitor how effectively they are changing inputs into outputs. Labour and capital are monitored by measuring their productivity.

$$\text{Measure of labour productivity} = \frac{\text{total output (per period of time)}}{\text{number of employees}}$$

Productivity is more difficult to measure for a service sector business. It is also difficult when a firm makes many products and output varies across the different products. However, it is still useful to assess whether productivity is rising or falling. If it is rising, labour costs per unit will be falling, making the firm more competitive. If it is falling, managers might have to:

➤ cut the number of workers

➤ increase the amount of capital

➤ use capital more effectively, e.g. increase the number of shifts so that machinery is running for longer each day

➤ improve workers' motivation to increase their output.

Capital productivity is measured by:

$$\text{Measure of capital productivity} = \frac{\text{total output (per period of time)}}{\text{capital employed}}$$

Advancements in technology and increased use of machinery have resulted in both capital and labour productivity increasing for many businesses.

Efficiency and stock control

Efficiency is the measure of how well resources such as labour and capital are being used. As well as by improving productivity, it can be improved by:

➤ reducing waste

➤ having a quality system that aims for zero defects

➤ managing stock levels effectively.

Stock (or inventory) can take three forms:

1. Raw materials and components

2. Work in progress

3. Finished goods

An efficient stock control system means managing all three stock levels efficiently, with the following benefits:

➤ Reduces storage costs

➤ Makes sure working capital is not tied up in stock

➤ Reduces damaged or out-of-date stock (due to mishandling or poor storage conditions)

➤ Ensures sales are not lost through inability to meet orders

➤ Improves image of business as orders are met promptly and with no financial penalties for late delivery

➤ Gains discounts for bulk orders

➤ Reduces idle time waiting for components to be delivered to production line.

Here is a typical stock control chart:

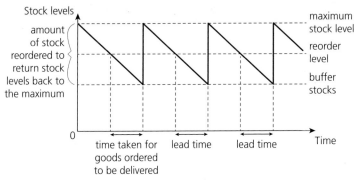

Buffer stocks = minimum stocks that should be held to prevent delay in production
Maximum stock level = maximum level of stock which can be stored
Re-order quantity = the number of items ordered each time
Lead time = time taken from order to delivery of stock
Re-order stock level = the level of stocks when a re-order is triggered

Just-in-time (JIT) stock control requires that no buffer stocks are held, and the finished products are not usually stored.

Case study

National Express sells tickets for coach travel between major cities in the UK for as little as £1. This automated operation has increased efficiency and made it easier for managers to organise coach routes and passenger pick-ups. Productivity per worker has increased.

Summary

Production is the using of inputs and changing them into outputs as efficiently as possible. This is to produce the maximum amount of output possible with this given amount of inputs.

Project management

A project is a temporary activity aiming to achieve a specific objective. Project management is the process of planning, organising, motivating and controlling resources to achieve this objective. Critical path analysis is a project management technique that uses network diagrams to simulate the dependency of project activities.

Importance of project management

Business projects can be relatively small, such as relocating a shop from one town to another, or very large, such as a high-speed rail project. Planning and managing resources is essential to the success of all business projects. Good planning and management should help to ensure that a project:

➤ is completed on time and to budget

➤ avoids waste and uses resources as efficiently as possible

➤ completes the activities in the correct sequence and with simultaneous activities identified.

Critical path analysis (network analysis)

Critical path analysis (CPA) is one of the most widely used project management techniques. To use this technique management must:

➤ identify all the separate tasks involved in a project

➤ estimate the duration (length of time) of each task

➤ understand the logical dependencies of the activities. This means knowing which tasks precede a task and which follow on from it.

Here is an example of a bridge-building project that requires the following activities to be undertaken:

Activity	Preceding activities	Duration (days)
A	–	8
B	–	6
C	A	12
D	B,C	6
E	A	14
F	E	10
G	F,D	3
H	B,C	14
I	G,H	3
J	I	4

The next stage is to draw a network diagram based on that information. Network diagrams show the logical relationship between all activities and contain:

➤ Nodes which are numbered

➤ Earliest start times (EST) of each activity – the earliest time that activities from that node can start

➤ Latest finish times (LFT) of each activity – the latest time that activities from that node can finish without extending the critical path and delaying the project

➤ The critical path – the sequence of activities that must be completed on time. There is no spare time on any of these activities. The path is indicated with small parallel lines.

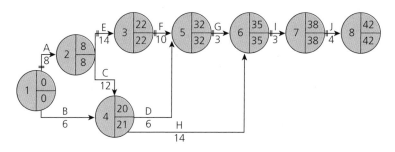

135

Uses of CPA

The CPA shows the activities that must be carefully managed for the entire project to be completed on time. Float times can be calculated for all non-critical activities.

Delays with any activity can be assessed in terms of whether they will affect the critical path, and how subsequent activities can be reduced in time to prevent project over-run.

Calculating float times

Float times are spare duration times on non-critical activities. This means that they could run for longer without delaying the critical path or later activities. Resources could be taken from these non-critical activities and used on critical activities to avoid potential delay.

Total float time for an activity = LFT – duration – EST

This time is the extra duration that this activity could last without delaying the critical path.

Free float time for an activity =
EST (next activity) – duration – EST (this activity)

This time is the extra duration that this activity could last without delaying all subsequent activities.

Limitations of CPA

➤ It is of little use if some activities are not included or durations are inaccurate.

➤ An accurate network diagram does not guarantee a successful project. Management still has to order resources and materials on time, manage them effectively, and motivate the workforce.

Gantt charts

These are used to achieve similar objectives to a CPA network diagram. They use a horizontal bar chart. Each bar represents an activity and time is measured on the horizontal axis. They indicate activities that can be completed simultaneously and those that must be undertaken sequentially. Here is an example:

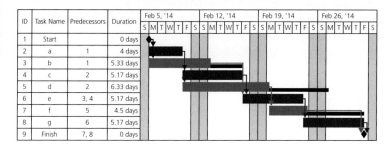

ID	Task Name	Predecessors	Duration
1	Start		0 days
2	a	1	4 days
3	b	1	5.33 days
4	c	2	5.17 days
5	d	2	6.33 days
6	e	3, 4	5.17 days
7	f	5	4.5 days
8	g	6	5.17 days
9	Finish	7, 8	0 days

Case study

The construction of the Olympic Park for the 2012 London Olympics was planned using techniques such as critical path analysis. It took seven years to complete. Skilled and unskilled workers, building materials, specialist equipment and thousands of other resources all had to be scheduled to arrive on time. A huge project such as this could not be managed effectively without detailed planning techniques such as network diagrams and Gantt charts.

Summary

All projects require planning and management. Time deadlines in completing projects are important and obtaining resources at the correct time is essential. Managing activities along the critical path and using float times on non-critical activities can help to achieve successful projects on time.

Quality

A quality product is one that meets customer expectations. It does not mean that the good or service is necessarily of the best quality possible but that it meets customer requirements and represents value for money.

Meeting customer expectations means that the firm's reputation and customer loyalty are improved, costs are reduced, and a higher price may be charged if appropriate.

What makes a quality product

If you paid £250 for a Mulberry purse you would expect the highest quality leather. If you bought a leather purse from a local market for £10, you would not expect the same quality leather. Your expectations would be very different for the two products but the quality should fit your expectations.

For some products, such as a Rolls Royce jet engine, the product must be perfect because of the consequences of failure. Products such as Zara clothes are often designed to only last the season. The level of quality expected from a product should be assessed by market research so that the business does not incur higher production costs making a product which is a better specification than customers expect. Keeping production costs competitive but providing sufficient quality is what the business is trying to do.

Quality is also important for service businesses. A restaurant which keeps customers waiting for food or serves food that is cold will soon lose its reputation and its customers!

There are two main approaches involved: quality control and quality assurance.

Quality control	Quality assurance
Testing or checking the product, often at the end of the process.	Certain quality standards are agreed for each stage of the production process. Workers are responsible for self-checking these standards have been met.

Quality control	Quality assurance
Advantages • Finds faulty goods before they go out to the customer	**Advantages** • Emphasis is positive, on producing fault-free products
Disadvantages • Only fault finding; does not build in quality	• Workers responsible for quality, which is motivating
• Expensive to implement as involves employing quality control inspectors	• Quality standards also applied to components bought in – ensuring inputs are of the required quality
• Emphasis is negative, looking for faults	• Relatively easy to trace back to where the problem occurred
• Products may have passed through many stages of production before faults are found – expensive to correct	• Reduces costs of final inspections and fewer returns of faulty goods
• Workers don't feel responsible for ensuring quality	• No need to pay quality control inspectors
	• Easier to achieve quality awards such as ISO 9000 (widely used within the European Union)

It should be clear why most businesses have moved away from quality control methods and to quality assurance.

Types of quality assurance

Total Quality Management (TQM)
This emphasises that quality is the responsibility of everyone in the business. Everyone has a customer to satisfy even if that customer is another employee. So implementing TQM means a total commitment to it by everyone; there should then be zero defects, eliminating the need for separate quality checks at the end of the production process.

Benefits are:

➤ Customer satisfaction from zero defects and therefore repeat sales

➤ Reduced costs for products not being faulty, repair costs, replacement costs and wastage

➤ Employees motivated from feeling valued, trusted and part of the business

➤ Reduced promotion costs as a reputation for quality will be part of the brand image

➤ Higher price possible due to higher quality

➤ Team approach to problem solving encouraged

➤ Employees encouraged to continually look for ways to improve their processes.

Drawbacks are:

➤ Training and development needed to change the way employees think about work and the business

➤ Only works effectively if everyone committed to the philosophy

➤ Possible equipment costs to check production at each stage of the process.

Benchmarking
This is where the best practice of the leading firms in the industry is used as a standard against which other firms measure their own performance.

A firm identifies an area of the business which needs to be improved. It then identifies firms within the industry which are considered 'the best' at this, assesses the way these other firms achieve being the best, then sets targets to improve its own weakness.

Benchmarking should be a continuous process so that long-term improvements in efficiency and quality can be achieved.

Quality circles
Small groups of employees from across the business meet regularly to discuss how quality could be improved or quality problems solved. This improves motivation and makes full

use of knowledge from across the business. All members of the circle must be committed to improving quality and confident that their recommendation will be implemented.

Quality standard marks

These marks or awards can be gained by firms and displayed on products to show that they are of a certain quality. Quality marks are often used to ensure quality for products associated with safety, such as the BSI mark for motorcycle helmets.

Case study

Harley-Davidson is an extremely successful motorcycle manufacturer and an iconic American brand. However, the company has had a number of problems with quality and reliability. Quality issues and increased competition from Japanese motorcycle manufacturers led to the company  being taken over. The new management implemented TQM and set about a new branding and marketing strategy to revive the bike's image.

75% of sales are from repeat purchases but loyalty is not inexhaustible and if quality continues to be a problem, sales revenue will eventually fall.

Summary

Quality is relative to customer expectations. It does not necessarily mean that a good or service is of the highest quality. A business can achieve quality by using quality control. Quality assurance is used more often than quality control. Certain standards are set at each stage of the production process and checking is carried out by all workers. TQM involves all employees in the business accepting that they are responsible for the quality of their part in the business. Quality is important for businesses to remain competitive and it can reduce some costs.

Technology

Technology in operations management involves the use of scientific knowledge, processes and equipment in industry. Advances in technology have had a significant influence on the operations department which produces goods and services. That influence has been felt in all three sectors of industry.

Technology in the primary sector

Technology has improved productivity and reduced the need for labour. Output is quicker, time is saved and waste removed. Farming, mining, quarrying, forestry and fishing all make extensive use of machinery to improve efficiency and reduce unit costs. For example, oil drilling now uses computer-controlled equipment to improve drilling accuracy.

Technology in the secondary sector

Use is widespread and includes the following:

Robots: machines with an arm controlled by a computer. Repetitive tasks can be carried out very quickly and accurately and robots have replaced jobs which were monotonous for workers.

Computer-aided design (CAD): programs used extensively in nearly all design and architectural firms.

Benefits
• Speeds up designs
• More flexible views of designs – 3D and can rotate the image
• Designs can be changed easily and quickly
• Fewer highly-paid designers are needed
• Programs can be linked to other software or even to the manufacture of parts on the production line

Drawbacks

- Expensive to install
- Training can be expensive

Computer numerically controlled (CNC): instructions for these machines are given by the operator. The machine carries out the instructions, controlled by a computer.

Computer-aided manufacturing (CAM): these are programs which operate robots or other automated machinery often used in flow production.

Benefits

- Production capital-intensive rather than labour-intensive, so lower labour costs
- Lower unit costs
- Productivity increased
- More flexible production as machinery is computer-controlled, allowing mass customisation
- Increased competitiveness

Drawbacks

- High installation and training costs
- Making employees redundant may be expensive
- Changing the nature of jobs may reduce morale
- Breakdowns can halt the whole production line
- Suited to flow production, so demand must be high

Computer-integrated manufacture: this combines CAD and CAM into an integrated process. For example, an order is received from a customer, the design department uses a CAD package to design the customer order, this is passed to the operations department where materials will be ordered automatically, instructions for CNC machines and robots are passed on to be processed. Finally the order is dispatched via an automatically-guided vehicle from the warehouse.

Enterprise resource planning: integrated business management software now ensures the flow of information across all aspects of the business from initial planning through development and manufacture to marketing and after-sales.

Technology in the tertiary sector

Examples include the following:

Financial services: sales of financial products such as insurance and pensions have become more competitive and information is easier to access via the internet.

Postal/delivery services: tracking letters or parcels has been made easy by using bar code readers in the delivery process.

Travel/tourism: bookings can be done online and tickets are electronic rather than sent by post. Online check-in has speeded up the process of travelling by air and costs are lower for airlines. Hotel reservations can be made online.

Advertising/films: there have been many advances in computer-generated imagery and special effects.

Print industry: technology allows newspapers and magazines to be produced using far fewer people and the editor can send the news stories straight down for printing on the presses.

Retailing: many stores have an online presence and some retailers only sell online. Technology has meant that payment is easier, either online or in store by self-checkouts. Stock control improved when barcodes were introduced at checkouts.

Information and communication technology: has led to faster administration and fewer staff required as banking transactions and invoicing have become automated. The use of spread sheets, databases, word processing and desk top publishing has revolutionised the way people work.

Benefits and problems of new technology

Benefits:

➤ Reduced unit costs

➤ Increased productivity

➤ Improved quality of products and services

➤ Reduction in waste

➤ Improved working environment

➤ Improvements in communication

➤ New types of jobs created which are less boring.

Problems:

➤ Some costs may increase, e.g. fixed costs of purchasing or leasing computerised equipment.

➤ Job skills change, bringing additional costs of employee training.

➤ Greater integration of processes and businesses. Breakdown in automated processes can cause chaos.

➤ Motivation may be lower if workers dislike working only with machines.

➤ Managing change and overcoming resistance to change may be more difficult.

➤ Unemployment may rise as some jobs are no longer needed.

➤ Hacking and viruses can cause major problems, e.g. identity theft. The Data Protection Act 1998 and Computer Misuse Act 1990 were passed to protect the interests of consumers and businesses.

Case study

Online electronic booking has meant
that flights can be booked online
directly with the airline. This has
speeded up the process and made
it much less costly to administer.
Previously, flights were booked via a
travel agent, who took a percentage of
the ticket cost, and paper tickets were

sent through the post. Also, the deregulation of US airlines has meant
many more routes and flights are now available.

Summary

Changes in technology have affected primary, secondary and tertiary sector
businesses. The introduction of new developments has led to enormous
increases in productivity and choice for consumers. However, there have
been some drawbacks to both businesses and the employees.

Business ethics

Business ethics refers to the use of moral guidelines to influence business decisions.

When business managers take decisions that they consider to be morally right, then they are behaving ethically. Sometimes this behaviour is referred to as 'doing the right thing'.

Importance of business ethics

Acting ethically means distinguishing between what is right and what is wrong and then making the 'right' choice. What is meant by the 'right' choice? Different business managers will have different views on this. What is considered morally correct or ethical differs between businesses and over time.

For example:

➤ Some investment fund managers consider the selling of weapons to be unethical yet many businesses still manufacture and sell weapons.

➤ In the past slavery was used globally; however, it is no longer thought to be a morally acceptable business practice.

The way in which businesses respond to moral questions is becoming increasingly important.

➤ Consumers are becoming more aware of ethical issues and expect higher standards from the businesses they purchase products from.

➤ Governments pass laws that lay down stricter rules regarding product quality, employee conditions and environmental protection.

Unethical decisions and illegal decisions

There are many laws that control business behaviour. For example:

➤ Setting a minimum wage level

➤ Controlling unfair competition (preventing businesses from making decisions with competitors to restrict competition)

➤ Restricting industrial pollution from factories.

If a business acts in such a way as to break these laws, it is behaving illegally. It would also be acting unethically. However, a legal decision is not necessarily an ethical one. A business might not be breaking the law, but equally may not be meeting expected moral standards.

Acting in ways that are widely considered to be morally right is important for most businesses. However, there are still many cases of unethical business practices. Here are some of the possible reasons:

Unethical business behaviour	Most likely reasons
Charging very high interest rates on 'pay day' loans (very short-term loans that are repaid on pay day) to low income people	• The lending business can make a high profit by taking advantage of vulnerable people in desperate need of money. • Low income people are most likely to be in need of short-term loans. • Banks would be unlikely to lend to low income people or for very short periods.
Producing goods in factories in countries that have no minimum wage limit and weak controls over health and safety	• It is much cheaper to produce shirts in Bangladesh than in France or Italy because there is a lower minimum wage. Most clothing producers use factories in 'low wage' economies to remain competitive. • Using low wage labour and factories with poor health and safety standards (such as no fire escapes) reduces production costs and increases manufacturers' profits.

Unethical business behaviour	Most likely reasons
Extracting minerals from low income countries with no established legal property rights for the local population	• It can be very quick and cheap to open mines for minerals such as copper and lead from countries that have no planning or property laws.

While it is clear that unethical decisions **can** be profitable, at least in the short run, many businesses do still choose to act ethically.

Benefits of ethical business behaviour

By acting ethically, businesses can gain some important advantages in spite of the fact that it could cost more in the short term.

➤ Consumers in many countries, especially higher income countries, are increasingly boycotting (refusing to buy) products that are supplied using unethical methods.

➤ Being seen to be ethical can be a good form of publicity, or free promotion, for a business. For example, Starbucks uses Fairtrade coffee – produced on farms paying above minimum wages – in all of its cafés. This helps to promote its moral standards.

➤ A business can receive negative publicity if its unethical behaviour is discovered. Negative publicity can lead to fewer sales. Ethical behaviour can lead to positive publicity.

➤ Often, the best and most qualified workers will prefer to work for ethical businesses as it gives them a higher status in society.

Ethical codes of practice

Businesses often attempt to ensure that managers and workers act ethically by:

➤ having a strict code of conduct which explains how the business expects its employees to behave in a wide range of situations

➤ using a team of senior managers who check to ensure that the code of conduct is being observed.

Case study

Primark, the UK-based retailer, claimed that it knew nothing about the use of children and 'sweatshops' to produce clothing sold in its shops, a practice highlighted in a BBC TV report. Primark dismissed several of its suppliers and repeated its commitment to ethical trading. On its ethical trading website it claims to be:

'Promoting better workplaces for those who make our products'

'Helping to build sustainable communities'

It is almost certain that other retailers in this competitive market are obtaining supplies from unethical sources but choose to ignore it.

Summary

Ethical decisions are based on moral guidelines. Ethical decisions and ethical business behaviour can be good for business, as well as for workers and the community. Unethical behaviour can lead to short-term benefits, but also long-term disadvantages for the business if it is discovered and made public.

CSR

Corporate social responsibility (CSR) is when a business tries to ensure that its policies and actions benefit the community and the environment. CSR is based on the view that a business should not operate solely in the interests of owners but should also consider the objectives of other stakeholder groups. It is sometimes referred to as 'Corporate citizenship', suggesting that businesses should be good citizens within society.

Examples of corporate social responsibility (CSR)

CSR can be demonstrated in many different ways. These are some of the most common:

Donations to charities

In many ways this is the easiest way to make a positive impact on society. Donations are a simple way for a company to enhance its reputation. Some critics argue that if business donations are from profits made in 'socially irresponsible' ways, then the businesses are just covering up the damaging consequences of their activities.

Examples of charitable support include the Ronald McDonald Houses which support families, and BP's funding support of the Red Cross organisation.

Community support programmes

In addition to making simple donations, many businesses provide long-term support to activities that help disadvantaged groups in society. For example, business employees may be encouraged to volunteer and become workers and leaders in the work of the charity. In many cases employees are allowed paid time off work to undertake charitable work.

American Express encourages its employees in Singapore to support the Association for Persons with Special Needs, and a recent development has been an ecology centre designed to empower people with special learning difficulties through environmental activities.

Supply chain management

A business needs to manage its supply chain effectively. This means ensuring that the suppliers of materials, components and services adopt the same CSR policies as the purchasing company. Businesses go to great lengths to ensure that their supplies are produced in socially responsible ways.

For example, Mitsubishi insist that all suppliers:

➤ do not employ forced or child labour

➤ have safe working conditions

➤ allow workers to join trade unions

➤ use materials produced in sustainable and non-environmentally damaging ways.

Environmental protection programmes

Nearly all large businesses have a 'green' policy. This usually includes strategies for:

➤ reducing waste and paper usage

➤ cutting emissions of harmful gases and energy use

➤ using sustainable materials that cause minimum environmental damage

➤ increasing rates of recycling and renewable energy use

➤ following all legal and regulatory requirements for environmental protection.

For example, Bovis Homes claims to exceed the requirements of all environmental regulations and laws when constructing new homes. It takes into account all biodiversity issues as well as the views of external specialists on protecting wildlife, ecology, woodland and historic features.

The growth of CSR

The CSR approach to managing business operations is quite recent. References to it started in the 1970s but it has grown into a very significant factor when businesses of any size take policy decisions and make strategic choices.

Here are some of the reasons for this growing significance:

Impact of multinationals: Stakeholder groups have become very concerned about the economic influence of the growing number and size of multinational companies and the impact they can have on society and the environment.

Pressure groups and media coverage: Groups such as Greenpeace and Friends of the Earth report on companies that they believe are acting in ways that damage the environment. These stories are spread by 24-hour worldwide media reporting and social networking sites. Bad news travels fast. The BP Deepwater Horizon oil disaster was reported around the world in a matter of minutes. Businesses also want bad news to be balanced out by good news – and CSR policies give them an opportunity to gain positive publicity.

Increased legal controls: There are laws and other government restrictions over business activity which is damaging to the interests of society – such as lower limits on accepted pollution and the use of renewable energy.

Creating shared value: This is the increasingly popular idea that a company benefits directly from the adoption of CSR policies both by itself and other businesses. Good publicity and potential increases in sales and profits can result. The whole business sector will benefit from a well-educated and healthy workforce and more sustainable use of raw materials, which could help reduce the impact of higher raw material prices.

Limitations of CSR

➤ Are company claims truthful? The social reports of companies make many claims for CSR benefits. External checks or audits on each company's CSR claims might be needed.

➤ Is CSR being used to cover up the damaging policies of the business? Some people think it is used to take attention away from the negative impact a business can have on a society or the environment.

➤ Acting in socially responsible ways can be expensive. Some owners of small businesses claim that they cannot afford to spend money on CSR.

Case study

Tata Steel is one of the world's largest steel producers, operating in many countries with different environmental and health and safety laws. Despite this, the central CSR policy for all Tata's operations is the same. According to the company's website, it is 'committed to a vision of creating value for all stakeholders'. An example is the creation of a Climate Task Force to reduce the company's carbon footprint by 20% within 10 years.

Summary

CSR is used by companies to demonstrate their responsibilities to stakeholders other than shareholders. It takes many forms but all policies are aimed at providing social or environmental benefits. CSR policies can be expensive but many companies consider them to be an essential part of how they operate. CSR has been criticised on the grounds that it is just a 'cover up' and is really a policy to increase business profitability.

Economic change

Change in the economic performance of the economy can have a great effect on business, to the extent that it can lead to business failure or great success. It is one of the 'E's in PESTEL (Political, Economic, Social, Technological, Environmental, Legal – external influences on business). PESTEL is a form of strategic analysis used in marketing and business development decision-making.

Key indicators

A country's economic performance is measured by key indicators of performance:

➤ the rate of inflation

➤ the level of unemployment

➤ the rate of economic growth

➤ the balance of payments account

➤ the value of its exchange rate.

A business needs to understand these economic indicators so that it can take advantage of opportunities which may arise, especially as a consequence of government economic policy changes.

Economic measures	Possible effects on business strategy
Inflation	Causes and effects of inflation:
This is a general rise in prices in the economy. It is measured by the Retail Prices Index or Consumer Price Index. The target rate of inflation is around 2% for the UK. This suggests that a small rise in prices each year is quite good for businesses and the economy.	• Increasing costs (cost-push inflation) may be caused by rising costs such as wage costs, or import costs due to a depreciation in the exchange rate. May cause businesses to increase the prices of their products, cut profit margins or find ways to lower their unit costs. • Increasing demand (demand-pull inflation) is caused by consumers increasing spending and trying to buy more products than the economy is currently producing. Firms attempt to increase output but find it difficult to recruit employees as other firms are doing the same. Wages start to rise.

Economic measures	Possible effects on business strategy
Unemployment This is measured by the number of people claiming Jobseeker's Allowance, i.e. those people who do not have a job and are actively seeking work. It does not mean all people who do not have a job, such as retired people.	It is caused by several different reasons, for example: • A recession and falling demand cause firms to get rid of workers. • Workers change jobs and register as unemployed for a short time. • Technology changes and jobs are replaced by machines. • A business fails to compete with foreign competition. Positive effects include: • Easier to recruit additional workers and less pressure to increase wage rates. • May cause demand to rise for some products such as cheaper foods and clothes. Negative effects include: • Many people have lower incomes. • May reduce demand for luxury goods and services such as foreign holidays.
Economic growth This is measured by increases in GDP (Gross Domestic Product), which values the output of all goods and services produced in the domestic economy in a year. A growth level of 2–4% is considered good for a Western economy but some countries, e.g. China, have seen growth rates of 6–10% over the last decade.	Economic growth does not happen in a steady upward path but goes through a trade or business cycle. In the growth and boom phases, demand rises and sales of many goods and services increase. Business strategy is likely to be one of expansion, with rising profits. However, in the recession and slump phases, demand falls for many luxury goods and services and businesses may incur losses. They will tend to delay any investment and expansion plans until the economy starts to grow again.

Balance of payments	If a large and persistent deficit occurs, the following economic problems may arise:
This is a measure of the value of goods and services traded between one country and the rest of the world.	• A fall or depreciation in the country's exchange rate • Lack of investment from foreign investors • The government tries to cut the economy's spending on imports.
Exchange rates	Fluctuations in the exchange rate change the price paid for goods and services in the other currency. It can be difficult for a business to plan for the prices it can charge and its revenue from exports. It is also difficult to know what price it will pay for imported raw materials or components.
The government may try to avoid large movements in the value of the exchange rate as it increases the risk of trading abroad.	
An appreciation of the currency means that more foreign currency will be bought for £1, making imports cheaper but exports more expensive.	An appreciation will help businesses which import components, raw materials or finished products from abroad as they will be cheaper. The opposite happens if there is a depreciation.

Government policies

The government has three main economic policies to help it manage the economy: monetary policy, fiscal policy and supply-side policies.

Monetary policy

The government influences interest rates and the supply of money. Interest rates are set by the Bank of England and are changed to keep inflation around its target rate of 2%. Increased interest rates have the following effects:

➤ Increased cost of borrowing for businesses which may reduce investment or put off their expansion plans. Higher costs may also reduce profits.

➤ Increased costs of borrowing for consumers. The main form of borrowing for many consumers is a mortgage, so increased mortgage costs mean that less money is spent on goods and services. Businesses may need to adapt their marketing strategy.

➤ High interest rates in the UK may attract capital flows into the country and the exchange rate may appreciate.

If the government wants to increase demand in the economy, it will lower interest rates and make borrowing easier.

Fiscal policy

This is concerned with the government's budget, i.e. the difference between income from tax revenue and expenditure on services such as the NHS. If the government has a budget deficit, then it is spending more than it receives in revenue and has to borrow the difference. However, if it has a budget surplus, it receives more revenue than it spends and so it can repay some of its debt.

➤ If the economy has low growth and high unemployment, the government may want to increase demand in the economy and so might spend more than it receives in tax revenue, i.e. it will run a budget deficit by increasing government spending and/or reducing taxes.

➤ The government might want to reduce demand in the economy when inflation is high or in the boom part of the trade cycle. Fiscal policy will mean that the government will run a budget surplus, i.e. it will gain more revenue from taxes than it spends.

Supply-side policies

These are government policies designed to make markets and industries operate more efficiently. They are part of a long-term strategy to help growth to be sustainable without causing inflation to rise. Examples include:

➤ improving education and training to improve skills

➤ reducing income taxes to improve workers' incentives to work

➤ making it easier to invest to improve productivity

➤ reducing red-tape (administration) imposed by the government itself.

Case study

Republic, a youth fashion retailer,
experienced trading difficulties in 2013
as a result of falling demand due to high
levels of youth unemployment and a fiercely
competitive market. Sports Direct has
taken over Republic and plans to turn it
around. Sports Direct keeps prices low for
its sports equipment and clothing. It wants
to broaden its product range but also maintain a high street and online
presence – a strategy which worked for them in tough times.

Summary

Key economic variables in the economy are economic growth, inflation,
unemployment, the balance of payments and the value of the exchange rate.

Governments try to influence these variables by using monetary, fiscal and
supply-side policies.

Environmental factors

Climate change and its potential impact are now affecting how companies operate and the products they produce. Environmental factors – constraints and opportunities – are concerned with the impact of business decisions on the wider environment and whether business activity is sustainable. It is one of the 'E's in PESTEL (Political, Economic, Social, Technological, Environmental, Legal – external influences on business). PESTEL is a form of strategic analysis used in marketing and business development decision-making.

Assessing environmental factors

By carrying out an environmental audit, a business can identify the:

➤ sustainability of resources for the product: whether resources are being depleted or are being replaced

➤ pollution implications of producing the product: production methods and the waste generated

➤ environmental implications of consuming the product: taking account of increased consumer demand for environmentally friendly products

➤ cost implications of being environmentally friendly: higher unit costs caused by new production methods

➤ cost implications of not being environmentally friendly: poor public image, or higher costs arising from procedures that raise pollution levels in local rivers

➤ legal implications of environment regulations: heavy fines for businesses found to be polluting the environment or local rivers.

Opportunities and threats

Opportunities if a business is environmentally aware include:

➤ improved public image, possibly leading to higher sales

➤ reducing cost of waste disposal by recycling

➤ sustainable production methods

➤ fewer fines from government

➤ pressure groups less likely to cause disruption to production or negative image

➤ voluntary environmental practices attracting less attention from press or government

➤ investment from sympathetic investors attracted.

Threats include:

➤ reduced competitiveness with products that are produced in countries with fewer environmental controls

➤ increased unit costs

➤ changes needing to be made to the product or production techniques

➤ possibly reduced profits in the long term if higher prices lead to lower sales.

Case study

Starbucks ensures that it buys coffee which has been grown using measures to protect the environment. The coffee must be of high quality but also have been grown where farmers protect water quality and conserve water supplies, reduce the use of chemicals and preserve the biodiversity of the area.

Summary

Environmental factors are external influences which a business considers when making decisions, such as which production methods to use. There are advantages in terms of the brand or corporate image of being environmentally friendly, but this comes at a cost.

Globalisation

Globalisation is the increasing integration of economies around the world. The process is not new but it has been accelerated in recent years by reduced barriers to international trade and easier movement of people and capital.

Effects of globalisation

Globalisation is forcing most businesses to become more international in their outlook. These are the effects:

More competition
National markets are open to competition from foreign businesses due to reductions in tariffs and quotas resulting from World Trade Organization agreements and the increasing role of free trade areas such as the European Union.

More opportunities
These can take three main forms:

➤ Buying from overseas suppliers: This allows businesses to purchase their supplies from the world's lowest cost producers or providers. There may be transport, quality and communication problems but these can usually be overcome and the cost benefits remain.

➤ Setting up operations abroad: The growth of multinational businesses has been one of the most significant consequences of globalisation.

➤ Marketing products in foreign markets: Selling to foreign markets can take place even if a business does not set up operating facilities in these countries. By exporting goods and services, businesses can take advantage of a much bigger total market, and they also benefit from economies of scale.

Marketing strategies

Global localisation (or 'glocalisation') means adapting the product and marketing strategy to local needs. McDonald's makes the Big Mac available to consumers in all countries it sells in, but most other menu items are varied to reflect local consumer tastes and culture. Although potentially more expensive than pan-global marketing, being sensitive to local traditions is the most effective way to enter new markets. This is especially true in emerging market countries with strong local cultures such as the BRIC nations (Brazil, Russia, India and China).

Pan-global marketing uses the approach of a common, standardised marketing strategy in all countries. This has the potential to be cheaper than glocalisation as there are economies of scale in packaging, labelling, branding and promotions.

Multinational businesses

Most large business corporations are now multinationals – they have production operations (of goods and services) in more than one country. It is claimed that Coca-Cola has now reached all countries of the world except Cuba and North Korea!

The growth in the number and size of multinationals leads to benefits and potential disadvantages for both the organisations and the countries they operate in.

Here are the main benefits and limitations to the organisations:

Benefits	Limitations
• Lower costs, e.g. labour	• Language barriers
• Access to raw materials and components	• Foreign currency fluctuations
• Access to foreign markets from new operating base	• Need to be aware of local laws and customs
• Diversifies production risk, e.g. if one factory is forced to close, factories in other countries can continue producing	• Different cultures – may need to adapt products and marketing to be successful
	• Increased transport costs
• Possible government grants and other incentives	• Communication and control more difficult

Here are the main benefits and limitations to the countries:

Benefits	Limitations
• Increased investment should increase GDP	• Increased competition for domestic producers
• Higher national output as a result of a new production facility	• Profits may be repatriated to 'home' country of multinational
• Jobs created directly and indirectly in domestic supplier businesses	• May threaten closure of operations unless government assistance is provided
• A proportion of the additional output could be exported	• Potential environmental damage
	• Risk of loss of local culture

International business and exchange rates

With the exception of the euro area, trading with businesses in other countries, and investing in operations abroad, involves currency exchange.

Exchange rates are determined by the relative supply and demand for currencies, and they change constantly. This causes problems for businesses that trade and invest abroad.

Appreciation

This occurs when a currency rises in value against other currencies. For example, if £1 bought US$1.50 last month, but now buys US$1.75, the value of £ sterling has appreciated.

Depreciation

This occurs when a currency falls in value against other currencies. So if £1 bought US$1.50 last month but now buys US$1.25, the value of £ sterling has depreciated.

Common currency

This is a currency used by more than one nation, the euro being the most widely used. The euro was created to remove the risk and uncertainties to traders, investors and tourists caused by fluctuating currency exchange rates. It is also part of a longer-term vision towards greater economic and political unity.

Case study

Many US corporations used to rely on pan-global marketing. Growing national concerns about loss of local culture and identity have forced changes in marketing strategy. KFC's menus in China contain mainly items tailored to Chinese palates and the restaurant decor is adapted to local designs. KFC have been so successful in China that this country now accounts for nearly 20% of total revenue earned from over 3,000 restaurants in 650 cities across the world.

Summary

Globalisation is creating threats and opportunities for businesses. More businesses are now adopting an international outlook, taking advantage of freer trade and easier movements of people and capital. Marketing strategies are becoming more geared towards local needs and cultures (global localisation). Exchange rates fluctuate, leading to risk and uncertainties. Common currencies can reduce these risks and uncertainties but can bring other problems.

Political factors

Political factors are external influences of the government on business decisions and opportunities. They are the 'P' in PESTEL (Political, Economic, Social, Technological, Environmental, Legal), which is a form of strategic analysis used in marketing and business development decision-making.

Political influences

Government influences such factors as which goods and services it wants produced (or not), health, education and the infrastructure of the country. It passes laws that affect business decisions. Government also uses economic policies to influence the state of the economy.

Political influences include the following:

➤ Changing the relationship with other countries, such as being part of the EU or banning trade with some countries. This may bring new opportunities for some businesses, but increases competition for others.

➤ Introducing initiatives on health matters, such as '5 a day' healthy eating, increased participation in sports, and stop smoking campaigns. These provide both opportunities and threats for businesses depending on the product or services they sell.

➤ Tax structure may change under different political parties. Some governments might lower VAT whereas others favour lowering income tax or corporation tax. Decisions such as these may affect what happens to demand for products and the willingness of employees to work overtime.

➤ Immigration policy affects the availability of particular skilled or unskilled workers. Caps on immigration may limit particular workers being able to work in the country. There may be changing demand for products from migrant workers, creating opportunities for businesses to serve niche markets.

➤ Levels of spending by the government on local and national services will vary. For example, cuts to local authority spending may reduce the provision of some services but may increase opportunities for private sector providers of services, such as care homes for the elderly.

➤ Laws may be passed that affect different aspects of business activity, such as employment, consumers and location decisions.

Case study

The UK government arranges trade missions to promote the interests of British businesses abroad. India is one of the fastest growing economies in the world and provides many opportunities for businesses to both produce and sell there. In 2013, David Cameron led a three-day visit to India  to promote trade and investment deals between UK and Indian businesses. An example of a deal was BP and Reliance Industries Limited, which together plan to invest $5 bn in India's gas markets.

Summary

Political influences are the external influences of government on business decisions and opportunities. These influences may provide opportunities for some businesses but threats to others.

Social factors

Social influences are changes in society that may affect business decisions as opportunities or threats, for example demographic changes. They are the 'S' in PESTEL (Political, Economic, Social, Technological, Environmental, Legal), which is a form of strategic analysis used in marketing and business development decision-making.

Changes or trends in social factors will affect both marketing and employment decisions. Examples include:

Social factor	Effect on society	Possible effect on business
Age structure of the population changes due to lower birth rate (from women choosing not to have children) and people living longer	Low birth rate reduces number of young customers and young future employees. Increasing number of elderly in the population.	Changing nature of markets and target customers: less demand for products aimed at young people, so possible threat to teenage fashion businesses, but more demand for products aimed at retired people. Changing nature of workforce and age of retirement: fewer young workers and increasing number of older workers. Management may need to change the way particular jobs are organised to take account of these demographic changes.
Health of the population	Unhealthy lifestyles lead to more obese people and long-term health conditions.	Possibly less productive employees as more time off work due to illness. Increased demand for products such as diet aids and medicines may provide opportunities for pharmaceutical companies.
Patterns of employment	Increased number of women working. Change to more part-time working and more student employment. Technological advancements lead to increased opportunity to work from home.	Greater need for flexible work patterns for employees. Demand for child care or crèche facilities at work. Job descriptions and job roles may need to change to fit in with flexible work patterns. Increased demand for products or services such as convenience foods house cleaning.

Social factor	Effect on society	Possible effect on business
Education of the population	Increased education of the population leads to more skilled and adaptable workforce.	Greater availability of skilled workers. Reduced training requirements as more skilled employees available. New ideas and innovations from employees.
Fashion and lifestyle changes	Changes in trends and fashion for particular products.	Niche products see increase in demand, e.g. for cycling products after success at the 2012 Olympics. Shortened product life cycle for some products as trends change quickly. Increased market research needed to anticipate trends, shorter life cycle means lower marketing budget.
Increased divorce rate	More single-person households.	Increased demand for smaller houses is an opportunity for house builders. Reduced household income leads to changes in demand for products.
Multi-cultural society	Wider range of cultures in society.	Opportunities from increased demand for products such as different dietary requirements.

Case study

In 2012, B&Q, the UK's largest home improvement retailer, received an award for being the best employer of workers aged 50+. It believes its customers benefit from the mix of ages and experience amongst its staff, and its older workers are a great asset as they pass on their knowledge and experience to younger employees.

Summary

Social factors are changes in society that may provide opportunities or threats to a business.

Break-even

If a business is breaking even, it is earning just enough sales revenue to cover all of its costs. It makes neither a profit nor a loss. The break-even level of output or sales is that number of units that achieves this equality between revenue and costs. This is called the break-even point.

How is the break-even point calculated?

If a manager wants to calculate how many units must be sold to achieve break-even, this formula can be used:

$$\frac{\text{Fixed costs}}{\text{Selling price} - \text{Variable cost}}$$

For example: An ice-cream van owner has daily fixed costs of £210. She sells each ice cream for £2. The cost of ingredients is £0.50 per unit. Each ice cream sold therefore makes a £1.50 'contribution' towards paying fixed costs. How many ice creams must be sold daily to pay for these fixed costs?

$$\frac{£210}{£1.50} = 140$$

If she sells **fewer** than 140 ice creams each day, she makes a loss. If she sells **more** than 140 ice creams each day, she makes a profit. Selling exactly 140 ice creams means that she **breaks even**.

Break-even can also be shown graphically. The graph opposite has been constructed for the ice-cream seller. It shows the break-even level of production at the point where total costs cuts sales revenue.

The key points in constructing a break-even graph are:

➤ The axes are labelled 'Units of sales/Output' (horizontal) and 'Costs/Revenues' (vertical).

➤ Fixed costs are horizontal – they do not vary with output.

➤ Variable costs slope upwards as sales or output increases – but they start from zero.

➤ Total costs are variable costs and fixed costs added together – so this line starts at the fixed cost level.

➤ Sales revenue is upward sloping, increasing as more units are sold, and starts at zero.

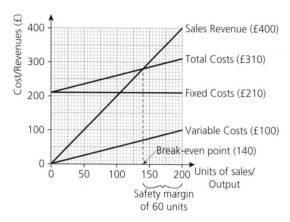

The graphical method has some advantages over the calculation method:

➤ It clearly shows the levels of sales at which the business will make a profit.

➤ It allows a comparison to be made between the break-even level of output and the current level of output. If a profit is being made, the difference between this and the break-even level is called the margin of safety.

How can break-even analysis be used?

➤ It is widely used by entrepreneurs when planning a new business.

➤ Managers can use it to assess what would happen to the break-even point, safety margin and levels of profit at different sales levels if certain decisions were made.

➤ Potential investors can use break-even analysis for comparing one new business venture with another.

Limitations of break-even analysis

There are limitations, especially when used by a business operating in a rapidly changing market or industry:

➤ Variable costs **per unit** are not always constant as sales or output increases. This would mean that the variable cost line on the graph would not be straight.

➤ The selling prices might have to be reduced to encourage customers to buy more than a given quantity. The sales revenue line would not be straight.

➤ Some output may not be sold so it would be added to stocks. The break-even model does not allow for stocks as it assumes that all output produced is sold.

Case study

The chief executive of India's Spencer's Retail business announced in 2012 that the company would break even in 2013. He expected sales growth of 15%. The business reduced fixed costs by closing some of its smaller stores and focused on the larger stores with rapid sales growth in non-food products. This allowed Spencer's to negotiate bigger discounts with its suppliers, which reduced variable costs and lowered the break-even level of sales.

Summary

Break-even is an important concept for all businesses at all stages of development. Any output or sales made above the break-even point will lead to a profit. Break-even point can be calculated or shown graphically. Break-even analysis is used to assess the current situation of a business and how profitability might be affected by making certain changes. There are some limitations of break-even analysis.

Budgets and budgeting

A budget is a financial plan for a future time period, for example the next financial year. In business, it can provide a plan for revenues, costs or both.

Budgeting is the process of setting and using budgets to exercise financial control. It is a key management task.

Why set budgets?

Budgets can be set for cost centres (sections of a business to which costs can be allocated) and to profit centres (sections to which both costs and revenue can be allocated).

Businesses and other organisations can gain substantial benefits from setting budgets:

➤ Senior managers know how much they can 'spend' and what is expected of them in terms of sales and profit.

➤ An overview of future finances is established and communicated to budget holders – people within the business with responsibility for budgets.

➤ All employees have a specific target to work towards.

➤ At the end of the year, the directors or owners will be able to assess success or failure as there is a quantitative plan against which to judge performance. This is done by calculating variances from budget.

➤ Finance is allocated to each department/division of the business.

➤ Budgeting requires coordination between departments in bidding for funds and this cooperation can benefit the operation of the business.

➤ Setting targets for each cost or profit centre creates motivation for all budget holders and their managers/workers.

➤ Managers and other staff can become involved in helping to set the budgets, which increases their status and level of responsibility. This is called 'delegated budgeting'.

➤ Budgeting is part of planning and encourages people to be forward-thinking.

How to set budgets

It needs to be done carefully. Realistic budgets will motivate the people who have to work within them. Comparing realistic budgets with actual results is a very effective method of assessing the performance of cost centres and profits centres.

Key points when setting budgets:

➤ Set the revenue/sales budget first – either based on last year's budgets or using market research data.

➤ Involve employees – they will feel more responsible for keeping to the budget.

➤ Use previous years as a starting point – but be aware of any substantial changes, for example increases in raw material costs or changes in economic conditions.

Variance analysis

This compares the budgeted figures with the actual outcomes. The **variance** is the difference between the budgeted figure and the actual figure. Variances are analysed in terms of whether they are favourable or adverse. A favourable variance is one that increases profit above the budgeted level. An adverse variance is one that reduces profit below the budgeted level. For example:

	Budget	Actual result	Variance
Sales revenue	£63,000	£60,000	£3,000 Adverse
Labour costs	£22,000	£21,000	£1,000 Favourable
Material costs	£6,000	£8,000	£2,000 Adverse
Fixed costs	£5,000	£5,000	£0
Profit	£30,000	£26,000	£4,000 Adverse

Looking at the table:

➤ Sales revenue was actually lower than budgeted – so the variance of £3,000 was adverse.

➤ Labour costs were actually lower than budgeted – so the variance of £1,000 was favourable.

➤ Material costs were actually higher than budgeted – so the variance of £2,000 was adverse.

➤ The combination of these variances resulted in profit being £4,000 less than budgeted – an adverse variance.

Management can now focus attention on the adverse variances:

➤ Why was revenue below budget? Were sales volumes down? Were prices reduced due to increased competition?

➤ Why were material costs above budget? Have material prices increased more than expected? Was there a large amount of wastage of materials?

The aim of management should be to investigate and act upon the adverse variances and learn from the favourable.

Limitations of budgeting

There are costs associated with budgeting such as the managers' time in setting and monitoring them. In large organisations, many people can be employed to set, coordinate and control budgets.

Budgets are rarely completely accurate as they deal with the future. This does not mean the budgets are pointless but it suggests that budgetary control is not an exact science.

Setting budgets can lead to conflict within an organisation as difficult choices sometimes have to be made.

Case study

Dell Computers has reduced its budget for IT maintenance by $150m, allowing a larger budget to be given to the innovation department. This does not mean that it expects less of its IT department which provides IT services to the whole Dell business empire with up to one million orders from new customers each day. By cutting costs and rationalisation, the operations side of the IT department has made significant savings.

Dell's annual IT budget is $1.2bn, of which $585m is now allocated to operations and $600m allocated to innovation and development – an increase of 30% in three years.

Summary

Budgets are financial plans for the future. Budgeting has many benefits, including better financial control and improved focus and motivation. Variances are calculated by comparing budget and actual data. There are limitations to budgeting.

Cash flow

Cash flow is the money coming (flowing) in to a business and the money going (flowing) out.

Money inflows can include payments from customers and loans received from banks. Money outflows can include payments to suppliers, salaries or wages and purchases of equipment.

Importance of cash flow

Cash means money which can be spent on a day-to-day basis. Without an adequate flow of cash – to pay wages, tax and other bills – no business can survive. It enters into a process known as liquidation. Other businesses it owes money to will want the business and its assets sold so that it can pay back the money it owes them.

The flow of cash through a business can be illustrated by a cash flow cycle. The longer the time period between paying for supplies and receiving payment from customers, the greater the risk of cash flow problems. Lack of cash is the single most important reason why businesses – especially new ones – fail.

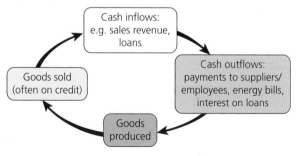

Cash inflows: e.g. sales revenue, loans

Cash outflows: payments to suppliers/ employees, energy bills, interest on loans

Goods produced

Goods sold (often on credit)

Simple cash flow forecast

As the consequences of running out of cash are so serious, businesses keep a record of the expected cash coming in and going out so that problems can be foreseen (anticipated) and, hopefully, prevented. This estimate of future cash inflows and outflows is called a cash flow forecast. One of the benefits of using a cash flow forecast is that it helps with future cash flow planning.

The inflows and outflows are forecasts – estimates made by the business owner of what cash income will be received and what cash payments will be made over this time period. They will be based on past actual figures or market research.

Here is an example of a cash flow forecast for a small shop:

All figures in £000s	Month 1	Month 2	Month 3	Month 4
Opening balance	12	14	11	3
Cash inflows:				
Cash sales	25	23	22	24
Total inflows	**25**	**23**	**22**	**24**
Cash outflows:				
Payments to suppliers	10	13	15	13
Wages	4	4	5	4
Rent and other fixed costs	9	9	10	11
Total outflows	**23**	**26**	**30**	**28**
Net cash flow	2	(3)	(8)	(4)
Closing balance	14	11	3	(1)

At the end of Month 4, this business expects to have a negative cash balance.

It is important to note that:

➤ net cash flow = cash inflows – cash outflows

➤ a negative net cash flow is shown in brackets on a cash flow forecast.

Improving cash flow

Method	Explanation	Possible drawbacks
Sell stock at a discount for cash	Reducing prices and insisting on customers paying cash to generate higher cash inflows	Might only be a short-term solution. Lower profit margins could mean lower profits in the longer term. Customers may get used to lower prices and not buy as much when prices rise again.
Delay payment to suppliers	Delaying payments reduces cash outflows and improves net cash flow	Payments are only delayed and the outflow will have to take place at some stage. Suppliers may refuse to supply the business if payments are not made on time.
Arrange a long-term loan	This will give a cash inflow and could give the firm 'breathing space' until other cash inflows increase	Interest will have to be paid – a cash outflow. The loan must be repaid – another cash outflow. This is an expensive way of overcoming a short-term cash flow problem. Unless the underlying cause of the problem is overcome, the loan will only delay the problem.
Delay buying equipment	Not buying new equipment to avoid a cash outflow	The equipment might have increased the efficiency of the business. For example, it might have been a new computer to assist with stock control or a new, more fuel-efficient delivery van. This equipment might have to be bought and paid for eventually.

Uses of cash flow forecasts

➤ Cash flow forecasts are used by managers to help plan financial needs, e.g. what additional purchases may be needed if growth is planned.

➤ They are also an essential part of a business plan.

➤ Banks will usually insist on seeing a cash flow forecast before granting loan finance.

There are some limitations, however:

➤ The forecasts may not be accurate as they are based on estimates and market research data.

➤ Using historical data means the predictions may not be current and are therefore not fully accurate.

➤ Forecasts may be produced by managers who are over-confident about the future.

Cash flow is not profit

It is important to understand that cash flow is **not** the same as profit. Here is an example of one reason why the two concepts are different:

Month 1	£000		£000
Revenue from goods sold	23	Cash in: Cash paid by customers for goods sold	15
Costs	14	Cash out: Payments to suppliers	12
Profit	**9**	**Net cash flow**	**3**

This business has sold some of its goods on credit (£8,000 worth) and customers will pay in later months, so the net cash flow is less than the profit.

Case study

Second Seed is a small shop that sells cushions, lamps, candles, furniture and gifts. Cash flow is a constant problem for small shops such as Paul's. The overdraft has risen to £18,000 and is needed for most of the year apart from the Christmas season. Stock levels are high as his suppliers often have a minimum order of six items. Second Seed has run a well-publicised sale for over a month with 30% price reductions, increasing cash inflow. Paul wants to develop the website for online sales and buy a van for deliveries of larger items. However, he might need a bank loan to pay for these developments.

Summary

The cash flow of a business means its cash inflows and cash outflows. A negative net cash flow means that outflows exceed inflows. Not having sufficient will lead to liquidation. There are several ways of improving cash flow in the short term, but they can have negative long-term effects.

Costs and costing

Cost is the amount that has to be paid to acquire or produce something. Businesses have to incur many costs both before they can begin production of goods and services and during production.

Costing is the process of calculating the costs that will be incurred (**how much** has to be paid) in order to produce a product or service.

Fixed and variable costs

Fixed costs do not change despite variations in the quantity produced or in sales. Examples include rent, leasing charges on equipment, salaries and business rates (local taxes).

Fixed costs often have to be paid before a business starts trading.

Unless a business makes just one type of product or service and operates from one site, it can be difficult to divide up most fixed costs between different products or sections of a business. If they cannot be allocated in this way, they are also called indirect or overhead costs.

Variable costs change as the quantity produced or sold changes. Examples include raw materials, energy usage in manufacturing and wages of temporary hourly-paid workers.

These costs are usually easy to allocate to a product, department or division. If they can be allocated in this way, they are also referred to as direct costs. It is possible to identify which product, department or division has incurred which variable costs.

Why is the distinction important?
Collecting accurate cost data and distinguishing between fixed and variable costs is important in:

Profit calculations: Gross profit is calculated before subtracting fixed costs but net profit is calculated by subtracting all costs from revenue (see: *Profit*).

Budgeting: Setting budgets for different departments requires variable costs to be allocated to the department. (see: *Budgets and budgeting*)

Calculating break-even point: The break-even formula requires fixed costs and variable costs per unit to be identified. (see: *Break-even*)

Making financial decisions such as:

➤ Should a business stop selling a product or should part of the business be closed down?

➤ Should a new order be taken or rejected?

➤ At what level should the price of a product or service be set (see: *Price*)?

Look at this example. A business manufactures three types of electric motor in one factory. Variable and fixed costs have been allocated to each type as follows:

2013 $000	Motor A	Motor B	Motor C
Sales revenue	50	75	90
Variable costs	35	40	60
Allocated share of fixed costs	25	25	25
Profit	(10)	10	5

Motor A makes a loss. Should production of it be stopped?

The answer to this question is almost certainly 'no' – at least in the short term. The reasons for this are:

➤ If production stopped, the fixed costs would still have to be paid and they would now be allocated to the two other products. This would increase the fixed cost allocation to B and C by $12,500 each, meaning both would make a loss.

➤ Motor A is still making a positive contribution, as sales revenue exceeds variable costs by $15,000. It contributes to fixed costs and profit.

➤ The allocation of fixed costs assumes that all three Motor divisions actually incur equal fixed costs. This might not be accurate.

In the longer term the business might be able to:

➤ close the Motor A part of the factory and reduce the level of fixed costs

➤ improve the marketing of Motor A to increase revenue

➤ develop a new product to replace Motor A.

Now look at this example. A hotel has received a request for conference facilities for one day and 50 delegates. The company organising the conference has stated that it does not want to pay more than $50 per delegate – $25 less than the hotel's normal rate. The hotel's conference manager has calculated the following costs:

Food costs per delegate	$18
Drink costs per delegate	$8
Additional labour costs to staff conference facilities	$1,000
Allocated fixed costs of hotel to each conference	$1,000

Should the conference manager accept to run the conference for the price requested?

No: It will make a loss if the $1,000 of allocated fixed costs is included. This is called **full costing**, or absorption costing.

Yes: If these allocated fixed costs are not included, because they will have to be paid whether the conference runs or not, then the event will make a contribution of $200. This is called **contribution costing** and is a very important method of taking decisions based on cost data. In contrast, full costing, which tries to allocate all fixed costs, can lead to inappropriate decisions being taken.

Other factors for the manager to consider before making this decision include:

➤ Are there any other clients who want a conference organised on the same day?

➤ Will it lead to other conference requests from this business?

➤ Will the other businesses that hold conferences at this hotel find out about the special price deal, and ask for a similar deal?

Economies of scale

Economies of scale are the savings made by a business as it expands, as production becomes more efficient and the average total cost (ATC) per unit is lower. They include:

➤ **Purchasing economies:** Large quantities of supplies can be bought at a discount.

➤ **Managerial:** Big firms can afford to recruit more experienced managers who might be able to increase efficiency.

➤ **Financial:** Banks may offer lower interest rates on loans to large, secure businesses with a good 'track record'.

➤ **Marketing:** A larger business is able to spread the cost of promotion and selling over a bigger output level than a smaller business.

➤ **Technical:** Large businesses are often able to buy the latest, most efficient equipment. Total costs will rise by less than output and ATC is reduced.

Diseconomies of scale

These are the opposite of economies of scale. Very large businesses can also experience increases in ATC from inefficiencies that arise due to their overall size. Possible examples include:

➤ Poor communication with lack of understanding of important messages

➤ Poor coordination between departments and divisions due to lack of effective working between them

➤ Low worker morale owing to the lack of personal attention and feelings of remoteness from senior management.

Case study

New business start-ups are increasingly using strategies to convert fixed costs into variable costs, as small businesses are more successful when sales and output are low. Some of the ways to do this are:

➤ Appoint self-employed staff who will be paid commission on each sale, not full-time salaried workers.

➤ Use outsourcing to other manufacturers rather than attempting to make everything in-house.

➤ Business services such as staff payroll, accounting and customer service can be undertaken by specialist external businesses who are paid per job done. The fixed cost of employing workers is converted into a variable cost.

Understanding the differences between fixed and variable costs can make all the difference between success and failure.

Summary

Costs are incurred by all businesses. Cost information is useful in finding ways to increase profit and in financial decision-making. Variable costs vary directly with output, while fixed costs do not. Total costs are fixed costs plus variable costs. Average total costs can change with economies of scale and diseconomies of scale. Businesses are generally trying to convert fixed costs into variable costs.

Investment appraisal

Investment appraisal is using numerical techniques and non-numerical factors to decide whether to spend money on capital projects. Investment is expenditure on a project – a new machine or building, for example – with the aim of making a profit in the future. Business managers obviously want to spend scarce finance on the projects that are most likely to be successful. The purpose of investment appraisal is to help them make these important decisions.

Numerical techniques

There are several numerical (quantitative) techniques that managers can use when appraising (assessing) investment projects. They all need the following information:

➤ **Cost of the investment:** For example, the cost of a new machine can be obtained from its manufacturers. However, bigger and longer-term projects – such as a new railway line – can be more difficult to 'cost'.

➤ **Annual net cash flows from the investment:** These have to be estimated and the further into the future the estimates are made, the less accurate they may be.

➤ **Life span of the project:** When a car hire company buys a new fleet of cars, it can be confident they will last for three years but the life span of other investments can be more uncertain. New technology equipment, for example, might quickly become outdated.

Managers analyse this data using the following techniques:

Payback period
This is the period of time needed for the net cash flows to pay back the investment. Here is an example:

A private gym is planning to purchase some of the latest aerobic equipment. It has a planned life span of five years. It is forecast to increase gym membership numbers by 5%, which would increase the net cash flow of the business.

Cost of equipment: £150,000

Life span: 5 years

Annual additional net cash flow: £50,000

The payback period for this investment is estimated to be 3 years (3 × £50,000 = £150,000).

The gym manager can assess whether this is too long for an investment project that will only last five years and can also compare this payback period with results from other potential investments. For example, the capital could be spent on refurbishing the café. The manager has estimated that this investment would pay back in just 2.5 years – and that the refurbishment would need to be undertaken again in five years' time.

Based on payback period alone, the manager should choose the café refurbishment. A faster payback has some important advantages:

➤ The faster the repayment, the lower will be interest charges on borrowed capital.

➤ Long payback periods increase the uncertainty.

➤ Money paid back in the short term has a higher present day value than money paid back in the longer term (see: *Net present value (NPV)*, page 189).

In fact, the gym manager would almost certainly not take the decision on the basis of payback results alone, because:

➤ the technique does not calculate profitability at all

➤ the payback period ignores the net cash flows after the payback period.

The gym manager would also calculate the average rate of return.

Average rate of return (ARR)

Also known as the annual average rate of return, this method calculates the profitability of investment projects. It expresses the annual average return on an investment as a percentage of the initial capital cost. This formula is used:

$$\frac{\text{Average annual return}}{\text{Initial investment cost}} \times 100$$

The average annual return is:

$$\frac{\text{Total net cash flows} - \text{Capital costs}}{\text{Life span of investment project}}$$

Using the gym equipment example:

$$\text{The average annual return} = \frac{£250,000 - £150,000}{5} = £20,000$$

$$\frac{£20,000}{£150,000} \times 100 = 13.3\%$$

This means that for each year of the life of the project, it will give an annual return or profit of 13.3%. The manager can now compare this with both interest rates and the ARR of other possible projects, such as the café refurbishment. This was expected to last for five years but the net cash flows were not expected to be constant because of:

➤ the slow improvement in sales in the first year

➤ additional labour costs as demand increased

➤ the expected need to spend more on maintaining the coffee machines from the fourth year onwards.

The expected net cash flows were:

Year 1: £50,000; Year 2: £75,000; Year 3: £50,000; Year 4: £30,000; Year 5: £20,000

$$\text{Average annual} \atop \text{net returns} = \frac{£225,000 - £150,000}{5} = £15,000$$

$$\frac{£15,000}{£150,000} \times 100 = 10\%$$

This result is now easy to compare with the ARR from the new equipment project. However, the ARR method does have limitations:

➤ It ignores the timing of cash flows. Money received in the short term is worth more than money received in the long term (see: *Net present value (NPV)* below).

➤ It does not consider the payback period.

Which project should the manager choose? The equipment project makes a higher annual percentage return on the investment yet pays back over a slightly longer period. The café refurbishment is less profitable – but pays back more rapidly. This dilemma could be solved by using the following third investment appraisal technique.

Net present value (NPV)
This method is based on the concept of the 'time value of money'. A sum of money received today is worth more than the same amount received in one year's time, for these reasons:

➤ Money received today can be saved in a bank at a rate of interest – making it worth more in a year's time.

➤ Money today is certain – future payments are always uncertain. The further in the future they are forecast to be received, the greater the risk.

➤ Money loses value over time due to inflation.

The NPV method of investment appraisal gives all future net cash flows expected from an investment project a value in today's money terms. It does this by discounting future net cash flows. For example, at a 10% discount rate, £1 received in one year's time is only worth 91p in today's money values – so the discount factor is 0.91.

Other 10% discount factors are: Year 2: 0.82; Year 3: 0.75; Year 4: 0.68; Year 5: 0.62

Using this approach, the net cash flows of the two investment projects above can now be discounted at 10%:

	Gym equipment: Net cash flows £000	Discount factor	Discounted cash flows £000	Café refurbishment £000	Discounted cash flows £000	Notes
Year 0	(150)	1	(150)	(150)	(150)	Initial cost–not discounted
Year 1	50	0.91	45.5	50	45.5	
Year 2	50	0.82	41.0	75	61.5	
Year 3	50	0.75	37.5	50	37.5	
Year 4	50	0.68	34.0	30	20.4	
Year 5	50	0.62	31.0	20	12.4	
NPV			39.0		27.3	NPV is the sum of all of the discounted cash flows less the initial investment

Based on this technique, the new equipment project is preferable. This is because, after discounting all future cash flows to their equivalent value today, it gives a higher NPV return (£39,000) than the café project (£27,300).

Non-numerical factors

Making important investment decisions does not just involve looking at figures and numerical techniques. Qualitative factors are important too:

➤ The attitude to risk of the management and business owners

➤ The impact on the environment

➤ Personal preferences, such as choosing not to relocate.

In all cases, the objectives of the management and owners of a business are likely to have significant effects on investment decisions too.

Case study

Reliance Motor Works (RMW) is a small family-owned business, looking to expand by taking over a car showroom. Finance will be from retained profits and a bank loan. The bank is insisting on some investment appraisal forecasts before agreeing the loan. RMW obtained quotations from building firms  and established that the capital cost would be £1m. This included a five-year lease on the site. Forecast new car sales – based on industry data – suggested that net cash flows of £400,000 could be achievable.

Based on these forecasts, the payback period is 2.5 years and ARR is 20%. Using 10% discount factors gives a net present value of £512,000. Based on this data, the bank was able to release the loan. The owners of RMW recognised that much of the investment appraisal data was subject to uncertainty, for example if the local economy worsened. However, they were prepared to take the risks.

Summary

Capital investments are always potentially risky – investment appraisal results aim to reduce the risk. The three main techniques used are payback period, average rate of return and net present value. Non-numerical or qualitative factors can also be important in influencing investment decisions.

Liquidity

Liquidity is the ability of a business to pay its short-term debts. A liquid business is more able to pay its debts than an illiquid one. Debts are paid from current assets – assets that are either in a cash form or can quickly be converted into cash. If a business cannot pay its short-term debts, it may be forced into liquidation by its creditors. That is why the liquidity of a business is so important.

What are current assets?

All businesses own assets. Some, such as property and equipment, are tied up in the business for a long time. These are called fixed or non-current assets. Other assets are used or can be converted into cash within a period of less than a year. These are called current assets. The three main current assets held by most businesses are:

Stocks or inventories: Stocks can be held in three main forms: materials and components used in production; work in progress (goods not yet completed); and completed goods awaiting sale.

Debtors or accounts receivable: These are debts owed **to** the business by customers who purchased products on credit. Most would normally be expected to pay within one or two months after the sale.

Cash: This includes money held on the premises and at the bank.

The key factor about current assets is that they are liquid, so they are available – or will be within one year – to pay the short-term debts (current liabilities) of a business. Without any current assets, a business would be completely illiquid.

What are current liabilities?

These are debts which a business must pay – or might be asked to pay – within one year. There are two main types:

Creditors or accounts payable: These are amounts still owed to other businesses or individuals that have provided goods or services on credit.

Overdraft: The bank could ask for this to be repaid at short notice (unlike a fixed-term loan).

How is liquidity measured?

Current ratio
Liquidity may be measured by comparing the total value of the current assets of a business with the total value of its current liabilities, using this ratio:

$$\text{Current ratio} = \frac{\text{Current assets}}{\text{Current liabilities}}$$

Look at this example:

31/3/13	Current assets (£000)	Current liabilities (£000)
Company X	15	12

$$\text{Current ratio for Company X (at 31/3/13)} = \frac{£15,000}{£12,000} = 1.25$$

For every £1 of its current or short-term debts, Company X has £1.25 of current assets available to pay them back. This is quite a strong liquidity position.

Now look at this example:

31/3/13	Current assets (£m)	Current liabilities (£m)
Company Y	60	115

$$\text{Current ratio for Company Y (at 31/3/13)} = \frac{£60m}{£115m} = 0.52$$

This means that, for every £1 of current or short-term debts, Company Y has 52p of current assets available to pay them back. This is a much less liquid position but it does **not** necessarily mean that the company will be forced into liquidation. If there is a steady flow of cash into the business, it will be able to pay its debts as they become due for payment – as long as all the creditors do not ask for payment at the same time!

Acid test ratio

A stricter test of liquidity for a business is to remove the value of stocks from current assets and then calculate the following ratio:

$$\text{Acid test ratio} = \frac{\text{Liquid assets (current assets} - \text{stocks)}}{\text{Current liabilities}}$$

Some businesses hold a high level of stocks as a proportion of current assets (such as furniture retailers) but other businesses hold a relatively low level of stocks (such as restaurants serving only fresh food).

No business can be absolutely sure that they will be able to sell stocks in a short period of time. They are the least liquid of the current assets. By excluding them from the acid test ratio, this gives a much more realistic test of the ability of a business to pay back its short-term debts.

How will the acid test results of Companies X and Y differ from the current ratio results?

31/3/13 £	Current assets	Stocks held	Liquid assets	Current liabilities
Company X	15,000	10,000	5,000	12,000
Company Y	60m	5m	55m	115m

$$\text{Acid test ratio for Company X} = \frac{\text{£5,000}}{\text{£12,000}} = 0.42$$

This is substantially below the current ratio for Company X, as it holds a high value of stocks compared to current assets.

Acid test ratio for Company $Y = \dfrac{£55m}{£115m} = 0.48$

According to the acid test ratio, Company Y appears to be more liquid than Company X, as it has a very low level of stocks compared to total current assets.

How can a business increase its liquidity?

A business with very low levels of liquidity may not be able to pay all of its creditors. The creditors could then force the business into administration, resulting in a selling off (liquidation) of all its assets.

There are several ways for a business to increase its liquidity:

Method	How it works	Limitations
Sell assets that are no longer required	Sale of assets will lead to additional cash for the business	If the assets are sold quickly to raise cash, the best price might not be received
		The assets might be useful in the future
Sell off slow-moving stock, e.g. by offering discounts for cash	This will improve the acid test ratio but not the current ratio – as one form of current assets is being changed for another	Selling stocks for cash at a discount will reduce profit margins
Good management of customers' accounts	Send out bills rapidly and ask for speedy payment	Some customers may move to another business offering longer credit periods

Case study

Liquidity ratios differ between businesses engaged in different industries. Consider these ratio results for 2012:

	Current ratio	Acid test ratio
Sainsbury's	0.58	0.3
Pakistan State Oil Co.	1.1	0.8

Supermarket companies often have low levels of liquidity as they employ very efficient stock management systems and have few debtors but often owe suppliers (creditors) very large sums. Most supermarket customers pay by cash or debit card. This helps to explain Sainsbury's relatively low liquidity ratio results; however, they do not suggest that it cannot pay its short-term debts.

Manufacturing and production-based businesses often have higher levels of liquidity than supermarkets. They can hold high levels of stocks. The Pakistan State Oil Co. holds stocks of oil and stocks of processed oil products as they pass through oil refineries to petrol stations and other end users. Most of the products sold by these businesses will be on credit, so they will have high debtor levels.

Summary

Liquidity is vital for all businesses, so that a business can pay its short-term debts. It is often measured using two ratios – current ratio and acid test ratio. Businesses in different industries have different levels of liquidity.

Profit and profitability

Profit is the surplus remaining after total costs have been deducted from the total income or revenue of a business.

Profitability is the level of profits made by a business compared to its sales revenue and capital employed and is used to assess the performance of a business. It is measured by ratios that can then be compared, both over time and with other similar businesses.

Importance of profit

➤ Profit **provides a return** to the owner(s) of a business for the risk they have taken in operating the business and the capital they have invested in it.

➤ Profit **provides finance** for the business to expand. In most businesses, much of the profits made will be kept (retained) in the business and used to expand it.

➤ Profit **acts as an incentive** for new entrepreneurs to set up in business or for existing businesses to expand.

Types of profit

Profit can be calculated in three ways:

Gross profit
Definition: Sales revenue (income from sale of goods and services) less the cost of producing goods and services.

Note that gross profit does not deduct **all** business costs – only the costs involved in producing and selling products, for example the costs of materials. These are also called the cost of goods sold. Here is an example:

Action Aerials Ltd sold 200 TV aerials in 2013 at £50 each, giving a total income of £10,000.

The cost of buying in the aerials sold was £4,000 (i.e. £20 each).

Gross profit = Total income – cost of goods sold

$$= £10,000 – £4,000$$

$$= £6,000$$

Net profit

Definition: Sales revenue less total costs (including all overheads and interest costs).

Net profit can also be calculated by subtracting overhead costs from gross profit. It is possible for a business to make a gross profit but a net **loss** if overheads exceed gross profit. On some company accounts, net profit is also referred to as profit, net income or profit before tax. Here is an example:

Action Aerials Ltd paid £3,000 in overhead and interest costs in 2013. From the example above, its gross profit was £6,000.

Net profit = gross profit – overheads

$$= £6,000 – £3,000$$

$$= £3,000$$

Note that net profit is always less than gross profit.

Retained profit

Definition: Net profit less tax and dividends.

Action Aerials paid £1,000 in corporation tax in 2013 and £1,500 in dividends to shareholders. From the example above, its net profit is £3,000.

Retained profit = net profit – (tax + dividends)

$$= £3,000 – (£1,000 + £1,500)$$

$$= £500$$

The retained profit is therefore left in the business to help finance its growth.

These three types of profit provide different information:

➤ **Gross profit**: success of business in making a profit on the cost price of the goods/services

➤ **Net profit:** success of business in making a profit after all costs have been deducted

➤ **Retained profit**: how much profit remains in the business at the end of the trading period.

Why measure profitability?

Profitability assesses whether the business is:

➤ achieving the objectives set for it

➤ performing better or worse than competing businesses

➤ performing better or worse than in previous years.

For example, look at the net profit figures of two retailing businesses in 2013:

➤ Company A: net profit £36m

➤ Company B: net profit £1.8m

This shows that Company A made 20 times the amount of net profit that Company B did. Now look at their sales revenue (total value of goods sold) in 2013:

➤ Company A: sales revenue £720m

➤ Company B: sales revenue £18m

Comparing sales revenue and net profit reveals much more about their relative success. Company A's sales revenue was 20 times greater than its net profit; Company B's sales revenue was only 10 times greater. So Company A has actually been more successful than Company B at turning 'sales into profits'.

How is profitability measured?

Profitability is measured by the following three ratios:

Ratio	How measured	What it shows
Gross profit margin (%) (GPM)	$\dfrac{\text{Gross profit}}{\text{Sales revenue}} \times 100$	Gross profit as a proportion of sales revenue, e.g. a 20% GPM means that gross profit of 20p is made on sales of £1.
Net profit margin (%) (NPM) (See 'Types of profit' for other terms for net profit)	$\dfrac{\text{Net profit}}{\text{Sales revenue}} \times 100$	Net profit as a proportion of sales revenue, e.g. a NPM of 10% means that net profit of 10p is made on sales of £1.
Return on capital employed (%) (ROCE) Capital employed is the total value of long-term capital invested in a business – long-term loans + shareholders' funds	$\dfrac{\text{Net profit}}{\text{Capital employed}} \times 100$	Percentage annual return (profit) on each £1 invested in the business, e.g. a ROCE of 15% means that each £1 invested in the business has returned 15p in net profit.

Here is a worked example:

2013 (All figs £m)	Gross profit	Net profit	Sales revenue	Capital employed
Company A	108	36	720	1,000
Company B	3.6	1.8	18	24

2013	GPM	NPM	ROCE
Company A	$\dfrac{108}{720} \times 100 = 15\%$	$\dfrac{36}{720} \times 100 = 5\%$	$\dfrac{36}{1,000} \times 100 = 3.6\%$
Company B	$\dfrac{3.6}{18} \times 100 = 20\%$	$\dfrac{1.8}{18} \times 100 = 10\%$	$\dfrac{1.8}{24} \times 100 = 7.5\%$

This shows that Company B is more effective at converting sales revenue and capital into profits, even though its **total profit** is much less than Company A.

➤ Company B has a higher gross profit margin – meaning that on each £1 of sales, it makes more gross profit than Company A. It either prices its products higher than Company A or has lower costs of sales.

➤ Company B has a net profit margin two times higher than Company A. Company B is much more effective at converting sales into net profit. Perhaps it controls its costs much more effectively than Company A.

➤ Finally, each £1 invested in Company B is used more effectively to make a higher net profit.

Who would find these results useful?
Owners/shareholders: deciding which companies to buy shares in.

Managers: comparing the profitability of their company over time and with similar businesses.

Limitations of using ratio results
All accounting ratio results should be used with caution because:

➤ companies have different accounting year end dates so the results are not always comparable

➤ ratios only measure financial data, not customer satisfaction, employee morale and product quality

➤ methods of valuing assets such as brands can differ between businesses, so capital employed data may not be comparable

➤ ratio results only focus on past results, although past performance can be a guide to the future performance of the business.

Here are some common ways to increase profitability:

Ratio	Ways to improve	Evaluation
Gross profit margin	Reduce cost of sales, e.g. cheaper materials	Gross profit margin is increased Consumers may buy less due to increased prices Quality may be reduced if cheaper materials are used
Net profit margin	Raise gross profit margin Reduce fixed overhead expenses	Net profit margin is increased It is difficult to reduce overheads without negatively affecting the business. Reducing advertising might cut sales; reducing administration costs might lead to less effective management
Return on capital employed	Increase net profit Sell assets, such as spare land, that are not fully used and repay loans	Return on capital employed is increased Although this reduces capital employed, the assets may be needed in future

Case study

Marks and Spencer is a much larger retailing company than Next. In 2012, Marks and Spencer sales totalled over £9.9bn – over five times more than that of its rival. In terms of profitability, Marks and Spencer recorded a gross profit margin of 7.32% compared to 29.6% for Next. The difference in the net profit margin was smaller – 4.69% for Marks and Spencer but 12.62% for Next. Comparing the return on capital employed ratios, Marks and Spencer achieved 12.46% and Next 16.3%. The management of Marks and Spencer will be looking very closely at these comparisons before deciding how they can increase profitability.

Summary

Profitability can be compared by using profit margin ratios and the return on capital employed. Although these ratio results are a useful guide to profitability, they do have limitations.

Shareholders' equity

Shareholders' equity is the difference between the total value of a company's assets and its liabilities. Shareholders are the owners of company shares. Assets are items of value owned by the business. Liabilities are debts of the business.

Shareholders' equity is also known as shareholders' funds or owners' equity.

Balance sheet

A balance sheet is a financial account that must be drawn up at least once a year. It records the value, at one moment in time, of all of the business's assets (items of value) and liabilities. The assets can be classified into current and non-current assets.

Current assets are stocks, debtors and cash (see: *Liquidity*). Non-current (fixed) assets include:

➤ property such as factories, workshops, offices, shops

➤ equipment such as vehicles, computers, machines

➤ intangible items (which do not physically exist) such as patents, trademarks, brands, intellectual property rights.

The liabilities, or debts, owed by the business can be classified into non-current and current liabilities. Non-current (long-term) liabilities are debts owed, often to banks, that can be paid back over a period of more than one year. Current liabilities are payable within one year, for example bank overdraft, creditors.

If a business has assets with a total value of £1m and liabilities with a total value of £0.6m, then the difference is called shareholders' equity or shareholders' funds. This is the owners' stake in the business. If all the assets were sold for their balance sheet value and all the liabilities repaid, this figure would be paid back to the shareholders as owners of the business.

Components of shareholders' equity

The two main components of shareholders' equity are:

Share capital: This is the money raised from the sale of the company's shares to shareholders. If a company is able to sell additional new shares for more than their nominal value – perhaps because the business has been successful – the additional value of these shares will be added to a 'share premium reserve'.

Retained profit reserves: These result from profits retained in the business from previous years' trading. The term is slightly misleading – reserves are not cash reserves ready to be paid out to shareholders. The profits retained in the business are nearly always spent on purchasing additional assets, so unless the whole business is sold, shareholders will not receive these reserves.

This example balance sheet shows a common way of presenting a limited company's balance sheet. The exact format can vary but all balance sheets must show the same information.

Jones Hotel plc. Balance Sheet as at 31/10/13
(Additional notes are to aid the reader's understanding.)

	£000	*Additional notes*
Non-current assets:		*Also known as fixed assets*
Property	500	
Equipment	125	
Intangibles	25	
	650	
Current assets:		
Stocks	18	*Also known as inventories*
Debtors	23	*Also known as accounts receivable*
Cash	2	
	43	
Total assets	693	*The sum of non-current and current assets*

Current liabilities:		
Overdraft	15	
Creditors	25	
	40	
Net current assets	3	The difference between current assets and current liabilities
Non-current liabilities:		Also known as long-term liabilities
Bank loan	150	
Net assets	**503**	Total assets less current and non-current liabilities. This must balance with total equity
Shareholders' equity:		
Share capital	100	
Retained profits reserves	403	
Total equity	**503**	This must balance with net assets

Increasing shareholders' equity

Shareholders, as owners of the company, will expect to see an increase in the value of their investment in the business over time. This would be indicated by increases in shareholders' equity. The two most likely ways for managers to increase the value of shareholders' equity are to sell further new shares and to retain profits within the business.

The second way raises an interesting dilemma. When a company is profitable, should the directors focus on increasing dividends to shareholders or increasing the retained profits of the company? Both decisions will increase returns to shareholders but in different ways. Paying increased dividends will give an **immediate** return to shareholders. Many of them depend on this income to assure their living standards. However, increasing retained profits will give the business more internal finance. This could be used to expand the business and earn more profits in the **long term** which will increase shareholders' equity and, possibly, increase share prices.

Case study

Rolls-Royce (RR) Group is the world-famous manufacturer of jet engines and power turbines. Its recent sales successes have led to the business becoming very profitable. Directors have been able to create conditions for increased shareholder value in three ways:

1. Dividends to shareholders increased by 8.6% in 2012 with a payment of £0.19 per share.

2. Shareholders' equity in the business increased from £3,975m in 2010 to £4,518m in 2011 due to retained profit reserves.

3. The share price increased from £6.00 at the start of 2011 to £9.22 in January 2013.

Summary

Shareholders' equity is the difference between the value of assets and the value of liabilities. Increasing it is one way in which directors can increase 'shareholders' value'. The most common way to do this is through retaining profits within the business.

Sources of finance

Business finance is about raising funds for business activities.

All businesses need funds or cash at certain stages of their setting up and development. There are many sources of finance and the choices of finance made by a business can be an important factor in the business's performance.

Why businesses need finance

Cash funds are needed by businesses for the following:

Setting up: New businesses need finance for the purchase of essential assets such as premises and to pay for operational costs until cash from customers is received.

Day-to-day operations: All businesses have to make payments, often on a daily basis, to pay suppliers and workers, for example. At certain periods of the year, for example in shops before Christmas, it might be necessary to hold a higher level of stock or inventories and the funds tied up in these has to be found.

Expansion: An owner wanting to expand a business needs finance. This might be for:

➤ Taking over another business: This is called external expansion and may require a great deal of finance.

➤ Opening another branch or moving to bigger premises: This is called internal expansion and will require finance for the additional assets needed such as premises, stocks and day-to-day costs of operation.

➤ Developing a new product: It can take several years to develop new products in an advanced technology industry. Long-term finance will be required before any returns will be received. The expenditure will include market research and product testing as well as the development of new technology.

➤ Entering a new market: This might be selling products to other businesses as well as final consumers, or entering export markets. Finance will be required for adapting the products for the new markets, market research and promotion campaign.

Sources of finance

There are many sources but not all businesses can access every one, for example, sole traders and partnerships cannot sell shares. Sources of finance are commonly classified into internal and external sources.

Internal sources
These are obtained from within the business. For sole traders and partnerships, they include 'own resources and savings' as there is no legal distinction between the owners' affairs and those of the business.

➤ **Own resources and savings:** Most newly formed businesses depend greatly on these. Entrepreneurs will have to put some finance into their own business before other investors or banks will commit.

➤ **Retained profits:** These are a very important source of finance. By not distributing net profit after tax to the owners (such as dividends to shareholders), finance is retained for the purchase of additional assets.

➤ **Sale of existing assets:** If an existing asset is no longer required, such as an empty shop, it may be sold outright. Alternatively, finance may be raised by 'sale and leaseback'. Under this arrangement, the asset is sold to a finance company that agrees to lease it back to the business. The business still has use of the asset in return for an annual leasing charge but it has raised finance from the sale of it.

External sources
These are obtained from outside the business.

➤ **Overdraft:** This can be provided by the business's bank. It is not the same as a fixed-term loan. Overdraft arrangements mean that the business can make payments for amounts greater than the cash balance in the account. However, interest rates can be quite high and the bank may insist on an arrangement fee. If the bank becomes concerned about the financial state of the business, the overdraft limit can be reduced or removed altogether.

➤ **Loans:** These are for set amounts over a fixed time period, usually more than a year. The rate of interest is usually fixed at the start. If the loan is for a property purchase, it is normally called a mortgage.

➤ **Grants:** Governments or institutions such as the EU may make grants available for a specific project, especially in areas of high unemployment. The Prince's Trust in the UK supports new business start-ups that pass certain criteria with small grants and loan funding.

➤ **Sale of shares:** This option is only available to limited companies. Private limited companies can sell new shares to family or business associates but not to the general public, so limiting the amount that can be raised. The owners can decide to convert the company into a public limited company, which can sell shares to the general public.

➤ **Business angels:** These are wealthy individuals who may be prepared to invest sums (up to about £1m) in a newly formed business with substantial growth prospects. They will usually insist on some degree of management input too.

➤ **Venture capitalists:** These are wealthy individuals or groups who invest in established businesses with growth prospects. These businesses may be struggling to raise capital from other sources, for example if they are operating in high-risk industries such as IT. The venture capitalists will expect to share in the ownership and the profits.

➤ **Sale of debtors' invoices to debt factors:** Debt factors are financial institutions that offer to buy the debtor invoices of businesses and provide immediate funding. They buy these at a discount to the face value of the invoices to reflect the risk of non-payment and the cost of the capital provided.

➤ **Internet 'crowdfunding' schemes:** These schemes encourage entrepreneurs with new business ideas to publicise their start-up on the internet and invite hundreds or even thousands of investors to contribute small sums towards the project. These relatively new schemes, which include Zopa and Funding Circle, are sometimes referred to as peer-to-peer lending.

Factors that influence the source chosen

It is important for businesses to choose appropriate sources of finance. This choice will depend on many factors. Often a combination of several sources will be used if sums required are substantial.

Factor	Why it is important
Legal ownership	Only companies can sell shares
	Only public limited companies can sell shares to the public
Existing debts	If these are very high in proportion to the total capital of the business (called a high gearing ratio), potential creditors will be reluctant to lend more
Purpose and time period	If finance is required to finance a long-term purchase, e.g. of capital equipment, then a loan or leasing contract is likely
	Permanent expansion of a company is often financed by retained profits and/or share capital
	Short-term finance needs, such as a temporary increase in stock, are much more likely to be met from short-term sources such as overdraft or debt factoring

Willingness of owners to give up some control	Business angels and venture capitalists may expect some control to protect their investment
	Selling shares to the public through converting a private limited company into a public limited company will dilute the ownership and control of the original shareholders
Interest rates	If interest rates are high, borrowing becomes less attractive as a source of finance
Existing assets	If a business has no assets that could be sold, other sources must be used

Case study

Different situations demand different financing solutions. Crest Nicholson, the UK house building company, recently announced plans to raise finance by 'going public' and selling 35% of the company in the form of shares. This will raise around £500m. Much of the finance raised will be used to pay off debts, buy out the stake of Deutsche Bank in the company and invest in more land for house building.

Spire Hospitals, the UK's largest private hospital operator, took a different approach when the directors decided a finance injection was needed. By selling 12 of the company's existing 38 hospitals – and leasing them straight back again – £700m was raised. This will be reinvested into improving facilities in the hospitals and paying off some of the substantial debts of the business.

On a much smaller scale, Robin and John Suave needed finance quickly when they decided to buy out the assets of a failed logistics business, Premier Logistics. Two main sources of finance were used to buy out the old business and expand its operations. The two owners used cash from their own personal credit cards and a large bank loan.

Summary

Finance is needed by all businesses for a variety of reasons. Short-term finance is needed for day-to-day operating expenses and long-term finance is needed to fund expansion. There are many sources of finance available and it is important to choose the most appropriate one.

Index